The Birth of Civilization in the Near East

THE BIRTH
OF CIVILIZATION
IN THE
NEAR EAST

HENRI FRANKFORT

Doubleday Anchor Books
Doubleday & Company, Inc.
Garden City, New York

Henri Frankfort was born in 1897 in Holland. He first studied history at Amsterdam University, obtained his M.A. in London, but returned to the University of Leiden for his Ph.D. He has done extensive field work in the Near East, his main project being the Oriental Institute of Chicago's excavations in Iraq from 1929 to 1937. Dr. Frankfort both organized and headed these excavations, which yielded much new information on the early history of Babylonia, from 4000 to 2000 B.C. In 1938 Dr. Frankfort went to Chicago to write and to teach at the University of Chicago, which had appointed him Research Professor of Oriental Archaeology in 1932. In 1949 he was appointed Director of the Warburg Institute and Professor of the History of Pre-classical Antiquity in the University of London. Among his other writings are numerous contributions to professional journals and a book, *Ancient Egyptian Religion* (1948). Dr. Frankfort died in 1954.

Cover design by Antonio Frasconi
Typography by Edward Gorey

The Birth of Civilization in the Near East was published by Indiana University Press in 1951. The Anchor Books edition is published by arrangement with Indiana University Press.

Anchor Books edition: 1956

First published in the United States of America by Indiana University Press

PREFACE

A FULL DESCRIPTION of the birth of civilization in the Near East would require a work many times the size of the present book. We have concentrated on the social and political innovations in which the great change became manifest. These bear most directly on the questions to which the appearance of the first civilized societies gives rise; yet they have received less attention than the concomitant changes in the fields of technology and the arts, the manifestations of religion, or the invention of writing. In so far as technological and artistic developments reveal social and political conditions, we have taken them into account; but we have not attempted to describe them in detail, and have kept our subject within manageable limits by a somewhat strict interpretation of the word civilization. While it is true that the terms "civilization" and "culture" count as synonyms in general usage, and that every distinction therefore remains arbitrary, there are etymological reasons for preferences in their use. The word "culture," with its overtones of something irrational, something grown rather than made, is preferred by those who study primitive peoples. The word "civilization," on the other hand, appeals to those who consider man in the first place as *homo politicus*, and it is in this sense that we would have our title understood.

A question which we have left unanswered is that of origins. The reader will find that in trimming the ramifications of historical beginnings we have exposed the trunks rather than the roots of Egyptian and Mesopotamian civilization. To what extent can their roots be known; what were the forces that brought them into being? I think that the historian must deem this question unanswerable. It can but lead him astray in the direction of quasi-philosophical speculations, or tempt him to give pseudo-scientific answers. It is the latter alternative which has done most harm, for time and again such changes as an increase in food-production or technological advances (both, truly enough, coincidental with the rise of civilization) have been supposed to explain how civilization became possible. This misconception bars the road to a deeper understanding. For Whitehead's words are valid for past and present alike:

In each age of the world distinguished by high activity there will be found at its culmination, and among the agencies leading to that culmination, some profound cosmological outlook, implicitly accepted, impressing its own type upon the current springs of action. This ultimate cosmology is only partly expressed, and the details of such expression issue into derivative specialized questions . . . which conceal a general agreement upon first principles almost too obvious to need expression, and almost too general to be capable of expression. In each period there is a general form of the forms of thought; and, like the air we breathe, such a form is so translucent, and so pervading, and so seemingly necessary, that only by extreme effort can we become aware of it.[1]

It is this effort which the historian cannot shirk, nor is there a short cut to the understanding of an

[1] A. N. Whitehead, *Adventures of Ideas* (New York, 1933) pp. 13, 14.

alien past; but I believe that the comparative study of parallel phenomena leads most surely to an elucidation of manifest and implicit form.

I have confined myself to Egypt and Mesopotamia, the cultural centres of the Ancient Near East; for in the peripheral regions civilization arose late and was always, to some extent, derivative. Egypt, too, was influenced by Mesopotamia during its formative period, but without losing its distinct and highly individual character. This matter of early cultural contact is of such importance for our problem that I have discussed the relevant evidence in an Appendix.

The following chapters are expanded versions of lectures delivered at Indiana University, Bloomington, in the winter of 1948–9, on the Patten Foundation. I am grateful to Dr. Helene J. Kantor, of the Oriental Institute, the University of Chicago, for generously providing me with the drawings for Figures 1 and 4.

H. FRANKFORT

WARBURG INSTITUTE,
   UNIVERSITY OF LONDON
17 DECEMBER 1950

CONTENTS

CONTENTS

LIST OF ILLUSTRATIONS

Following page 64

I. THE STUDY OF

ANCIENT CIVILIZATIONS

OUR SUBJECT is the birth of civilization in the Near East. We shall not, therefore, consider the question how civilization in the abstract became possible. I do not think there is an answer to that question; in any case it is a philosophical rather than a historical one. But it may be said that the material we are going to discuss has a unique bearing on it all the same. For the emergence of Egyptian and Mesopotamian civilization has some claim to being considered as the birth of civilization in a general sense. It is true that the transition from primitive to civilized conditions has happened more than once; but the change has mostly been induced—or at least furthered—by contact with more advanced foreigners. We know of only three instances where the event may have been spontaneous: in the ancient Near East, in China, and in South and Middle America. However, the genesis of the Maya and Inca civilizations is obscure, and for China we must count with the possibility—some would say the likelihood— of a stimulus from the West. But no appeal to foreign influence can explain the emergence of civilized societies in Egypt and Mesopotamia, since these lands were the first to rise above a universal level of primitive existence.

In the sequel we shall leave this aspect of our subject to one side: in other words, though the fact that in the Near East civilization arose spontaneously, and for the first time imparts a particular weight and splendour to the events, we are specifically concerned with the events themselves. And here, at the very outset, a difficulty must be faced.

It seems easy to deal in a general way with civilizations as entities; at least this is commonly done. Arnold Toynbee, in his *Study of History*, distinguishes without hesitation twenty-one civilizations—" specimens of the species," belonging to the " genus societies "—by what he believes to be an empirical method. But consider the problem which arises when we want to study the genesis of any one civilization in particular! We cannot merely assume that it is an entity and has a recognizable character of its own; we are bound to make that character explicit in order that we may decide *when* and *where* it emerged.

This problem is hardly ever envisaged by those who are best acquainted with the actual remains of antiquity. The archaeologist is either occupied with disentangling successive phases in his stratified material; or he constructs from his finds a fairly continuous story of man's increasing skill and enterprise. In this context the questions *when* and *why* we are entitled to speak of the existence of Egyptian or Sumerian (*i.e.* early Mesopotamian) civilization seem of secondary importance. On the other hand, the philologist does not encounter the question at all. For him, Sumerian or Egyptian civilization exists from the moment when texts were written in these languages.

Our problem is pre-eminently a historical one, and it has, accordingly, two aspects: that of *identity* and that of *change*. What constitutes the individuality of a civilization, its recognizable character, its identity which is maintained throughout the successive stages of its existence? What, on the other hand, are the changes differentiating one stage from the next? We are not, of course, looking for a formula; the character of a civilization is far too elusive to be reduced to a catchword. We recognize it in a certain coherence among its various manifestations, a certain consistency in its orientation, a certain cultural " style " which shapes its political and its judicial institutions, its art as well as its literature, its religion as well as its morals. I propose to call this elusive identity of a civilization its " form." It is this " form " which is never destroyed although it changes in the course of time. And it changes partly as a result of inherent factors—development—partly as a result of external forces—historical incidents. I propose to call the total of these changes the " dynamics " of a civilization.

The interplay of form and dynamics constitutes the history of a civilization and raises the question—which lies outside our present inquiry—to what extent the form of a civilization may determine its destiny.

For the moment, the distinction of form and dynamics enables us to bring some clarity into the problems connected with our present subject, the birth of Near Eastern civilization. Under the aspect of " form " we may ask: what actually does appear when this civilization comes into being? Is its form established piecemeal? If so, whence comes the coherence which characterizes it throughout its historical existence? Under the aspect of " dynamics " we may ask: is the emergence of this civilization a gradual process? Are earlier elements transmuted or combined by degrees, or is the peculiar coherence of a mature civilization the outcome of a sudden and intense change, a crisis in which its form—undeveloped but potentially a whole—crystallizes out, or rather, is born? The title of this book indicates the answer which I think the evidence compels us to accept as correct. But, before we consider the evidence, it will be profitable to discuss certain current opinions. For if it is true—as we have said before—that those best acquainted with the ancient Near East have rarely found occasion to consider our problem, it is equally true, of course, that we are not the first to discuss it.

Curiously enough, the two men who have devoted their life's work to the problem of the genesis of civilization have done so under a compelling awareness of its decline. Oswald Spengler and Arnold Toynbee both wrote under the shadow of an impending world war; and their work is, to some extent, warped by their preoccupation with decay. Oswald Spengler's *Decline of the West* was first published in 1917 and bears the subtitle, *Outline of a Morphology of World History*.[1] This indicates that the aspect of form (as we have called it) is fully considered in his work. In this resides, as a matter of fact, the element of lasting worth of his sensational, arrogant, and pompous volumes. They were written as a reaction against the prevalent view of history which was prejudiced in two respects: it considered world history exclusively from the western standpoint; and it presumed, with evolutionary optimism, that history exemplified the progress of humanity. For Spengler the word "humanity" is merely an empty phrase. The great civilizations are unconnected. They are self-contained organisms of so individual a nature that people who belong to one cannot understand the achievements and modes of thought of another. He maintains that not even in science does knowledge show accumulations transcending the limits of one civilization.

It would seem that under such conditions world

[1] O. Spengler, *Der Untergang des Abendlandes* (München, 1920).

history is not feasible at all, and this has, in fact, been maintained by no less a historian than Ernst Troeltsch.[2] But Spengler thinks otherwise because he applies biological methods to the study of civilizations. The very word "morphology," which figures in his sub-title, usually denotes the study of form and structure in plants and animals; it warns us to expect biological categories and these, indeed, abound. For instance, Spengler maintains that in different civilizations we can find not *analogues*—features similar as regards function—but only *homologues*—features similar as regards form. He also maintains that the life-cycle of each civilization runs through the same phases: youth, maturity, and senescence. This implies that a comparison of corresponding phases in different civilizations may be instructive, but that it is merely confusing to compare phases which do not correspond; for then one is led to expect, for instance, that an ageing civilization (like our own) might yet be able to produce great poetry or a live religion, which are features peculiar to civilizations in their youthful stage.

The birth of civilization is succinctly described by Spengler in the following passage:

It comes into flower on the soil of a precisely definable region, to which it remains linked with a plant-like attachment. A civilization dies when it has realized the sum total of its potentialities in the guise of peoples, languages, theologies, arts, states, sciences.[3]

I have omitted certain untranslatable references to an *urseelenhafter Zustand* from which civilizations are supposed to emerge and to which their "souls" return. For the quotation shows clearly that Spengler, not-

[2] "Der Aufbau der europäischen Kulturgeschichte," in Schmoller's *Jahrbuch ür Gesetzgebung, Verwaltung und Volkswirtschaft im Deutschen Reiche*, XLIV (1920), 633 ff.

[3] O. Spengler, *op. cit.*, I, 153.

withstanding these irrational additions, writes, like Toynbee, under the spell of the nineteenth century and attempts to interpret history in the terms of science. Even if we admit that the country in which a civilization arises influences its form, we must balk at Spengler's formulation (repeated elsewhere in his work, *e.g.* I, 29) which approaches materialistic determinism. By interpreting the harmony between each civilization and its natural setting in this manner, he denies a freedom of the human spirit which—to name but one instance—the achievements of the Greeks in Sicily and southern Italy splendidly vindicate.

In describing the death of a civilization Spengler is likewise under the spell of scientific notions. This is not obvious; in fact, Spengler's success is largely due to the plausibility of some of his most imaginative statements. We feel that it makes sense, even that it is illuminating, to speak of a youthful, or ageing, or dying civilization. But for Spengler such phrases are not metaphors; and when he speaks (as in the previous quotation) of a civilization's dying "when it has realized the sum total of its potentialities," he believes that he refers to a state of affairs as inevitable and as accurately predictable as the withering of a plant. He actually calls civilizations "living beings of the highest order,"[4] and he undertakes to state with precision which phenomena characterize each stage in their lifecycle. For him, an imperialistic and socialistic order follow a traditional and hierarchical society; expanding technique and trade follow greatness in art, music, and literature as certainly as the dispersal of the seeds follows the maturing of a plant which will never flower again. But to take the biological metaphor literally, to grant in this manner reality to an image, is not morphology but mythology; and it is belief, not knowl-

[4] O. Spengler, *op. cit.*, I, 29.

edge, which induces Spengler to deny the freedom of the spirit and the unpredictability of human behaviour.

Spengler substitutes the mystery of natural life for the dynamics of history which he, therefore, fails entirely to explain.[5] But to the aspect of "form" he has done justice as few before him. Here too, however, he goes much too far. It is one thing to stress the singularity of each great epoch of the past as a prerequisite of deeper understanding, and quite another to declare the discontinuity of cultural achievements to be absolute. Had the first been Spengler's intention, no one who had once comprehended the uniqueness of a historical situation, a work of art, or an institution, would have quarrelled with his dictum: "Each civilization has its own possibilities of expression, which appear, mature and wither, and never recur."[6] When he states, furthermore, "I see in world-history the image of a perennial configuration and transfiguration, a wonderful formation and dissolution of organic forms. The professional historian, however, sees in it the image of a tape-worm which tirelessly puts forth period after period," there is enough truth in this scathing remark for it to strike home. It is a negative truth, but it is born of a true perception of the poverty of our usual view of history as an evolutionary process. This view encourages us to project the axioms, habits of thought, and norms of the present day into the past, which, as a result, seems to contain little that is unfamiliar to us. It is remarkable how rarely historians of ancient or alien civilizations have guarded themselves against

---

[5] Spengler's position is invalidated in his own terms by Bergson's criticism of a deterministic view of life in nature.

[6] O. Spengler, *ibid.* Leopold von Ranke has expressed a similar idea in the splendid and simple phrase, "Alle Epochen sind unmittelbar zu Gott."

that danger. In this respect Herodotus was more perspicacious; he realized that the values of different cultures may be incommensurate when he frankly epitomized his description of Ancient Egypt in the statement that its laws and customs were, on the whole, the opposite of those of the rest of mankind.[7] This peculiar integration of the facts satisfied a Greek facing Barbarians. We, however, seek understanding. We can be resigned neither to registering astonishment nor to accepting the solution which a misconceived regard for objectivity sometimes proposes: a mere chronicling of the facts. We cannot rest content when we know that the Egyptians considered their king a god, entombed him in a pyramid, buried cats and dogs, and mummified their dead. We want to recover the cultural " form " in which these odd phenomena find their proper place and meaning. But it is a laborious, and never completed, task to rediscover the original coherence of a past mode of life from the surviving remains. Spengler attempts short cuts; overrating the extent of his truly remarkable erudition, and, for the rest, trusting recklessly his intuition, he forces the evidence to fit the schemata which he has conceived. He describes, for instance, the bearer of Egyptian civilization as follows:

The Egyptian soul—pre-eminently gifted for and inclined towards history, striving with primeval passion towards the infinite—experienced past and future as its entire universe, and the present . . . but as a narrow borderland between two measureless distances. The Egyptian civilization is an embodiment of concern—the soul's correlate of distance—concern with the future, manifest in the choice of granite and basalt as the material for sculpture, in the engraved documents, in the elaboration of a masterly system of administration and a net of irrigation works; of necessity a

' *History*, II, 35.

concern with the past is linked with this concern for the future.[8]

I hold this image of ancient Egypt evoked by Spengler to be totally at variance with the evidence. I have recently interpreted this evidence and described how (to take up the points raised by Spengler) the Egyptians had very little sense of history or of past and future. For they conceived their world as essentially static and unchanging. It had gone forth complete from the hands of the Creator. Historical incidents were, consequently, no more than superficial disturbances of the established order, or recurring events of never-changing significance. The past and the future— far from being a matter of concern—were wholly implicit in the present; and the odd facts enumerated above—the divinity of animals and kings, the pyramids, mummification—as well as several other and seemingly unrelated features of Egyptian civilization—its moral maxims, the forms peculiar to its poetry and prose— can all be understood as a result of a basic conviction that only the changeless is truly significant.[9] I do not offer this summary as a formula by means of which Egyptian civilization becomes comprehensible, for it explains nothing by itself and does not pretend to re-

[8] O. Spengler, *op. cit.*, I, 15. Incidentally, this quotation illustrates the very point at issue by emphasizing the almost insuperable difficulty of formulating an alien mode of thought. In transposing the words of a German contemporary I have been obliged to blur his thoughts and lose shades of meaning at almost every step: *Seele, eminent historisch veranlagt, urweltliche Leidenschaft, Sorge,* derive their overtones and deepest meaning from a world of thought which includes, at the very least, German literature of the romantic period; these terms, therefore, hardly bear translating. It is obvious that the disparity of terms and concepts is immeasurably greater where an ancient civilization is concerned.

[9] See my *Ancient Egyptian Religion,* New York, 1948, and *Kingship and the Gods,* Chicago, 1948.

place the detailed and concrete description of Egyptian life and thought which it summarizes. Nor can even such a detailed description ever be final or entirely comprehensive. I do hold that a viewpoint whence many seemingly unrelated facts are seen to acquire meaning and coherence is likely to represent a historical reality; at least, I know of no better definition of historical truth. But each new insight discloses new complexities which now demand elucidation, while at all times a number of facts are likely to remain outside any network to be established. However, if our view is true as far as it goes, then Spengler's view is baseless.

Spengler's lack of respect for the phenomena has a twofold cause. It is due in part to his overweening conceit, in part to his lack of experience. Like Toynbee, he is truly familiar only with classical antiquity and its western descendant. His *Urmensch*, his "primordial man," is the Greek or the Aryan Indian.[10] He ignores altogether the work of those who have ventured outside the familiar in order to meet an alien spirit on its own terms—the anthropologists, or, more precisely, the ethnologists or cultural anthropologists. These scholars have come up against behaviour defying every modern norm in their personal contact with primitive peoples, and in their encounters discovered an approach to the study of alien cultures which the historian of antiquity would be wise to make his own. The ethnologist will not take for granted savage customs and usages which seem comprehensible—even familiar—to him. For he has observed that cultural traits cannot be studied in isolation since they are integral parts of a whole—the given civilization—and derive their meaning from the particular whole in which they occur. Ruth Benedict,

[10] O. Spengler, *op. cit.*, I, 224 f.

in her lucid *Patterns of Culture,* states the case as follows:

It is in cultural life as it is in speech: selection is the prime necessity. . . . We must imagine a great arc on which are ranged the possible interests provided either by the human age-cycle or by the environment or by man's various activities. A culture that capitalized even a considerable proportion of these would be as unintelligible as a language that used all the clicks, all the glottal stops, all the labials, dentals, sibilants and gutturals from voiceless to voiced, and from oral to nasal. Its identity as a culture depends upon the selection of some segments of this arc. Every human society everywhere has made such a selection in its cultural institutions. Each, from the point of view of another, ignores fundamentals and exploits irrelevancies. One culture hardly recognizes monetary values; another has made them fundamental in every field of behaviour. In one society technology is unbelievably slighted even in those aspects of life which seem necessary to ensure survival; in another, equally simple, technological achievements are complex and fitted with admirable nicety to the situation. One builds an enormous cultural superstructure upon adolescence, one upon death, one upon afterlife.[11]

Hence—and as a warning to those who are partial to utilitarian explanations: " The importance of an institution in a culture gives no direct indication of its usefulness or its inevitability,"[12] for cultural behaviour is integrated and the whole determines the significance of the parts:

Within each culture there come into being characteristic purposes not necessarily shared by other types of society. In obedience to these purposes each people further and

[11] Ruth Benedict, *Patterns of Culture* (New York, 1934), 23–4.

[12] *Ibid.,* 250.

further consolidates its experience . . . and the most ill-assorted acts become characteristic of its peculiar goals, often by the most unlikely metamorphoses. The form that these acts take we can understand only by understanding first the emotional and intellectual mainsprings of that society.[13]

We have seen that any society selects some segment of the arc of possible human behaviour, and in so far as it achieves integration its institutions tend to further the expression of its selected segment and to inhibit the opposite expressions.[14]

There is, in this last passage, a suggestion of the dynamics of the formation of a civilization but it is not this aspect but that of " form " which prevails in the work of Benedict or Malinowski. For modern savages are relatively stagnant if we discount the disturbances caused by the white man. Hence the title *Patterns of Culture*.

It is, however, precisely the problem of the dynamics of cultural change—a problem misconstrued by Spengler and rightly ignored by Ruth Benedict—which lies at the centre of Arnold Toynbee's work. The first three volumes of *A Study of History* appeared in 1934, a second group of three in 1939, and a final group is still to be published. But we are told that the preoccupation from which the work has sprung, goes back as far as 1911, when Toynbee travelled in Crete and saw the newly discovered remains of the sea-empire of Minos. Then he chanced on the ruins of a Venetian villa, remnant of the time when Venice had dominated the Mediterranean with its galleys. And Toynbee was disconcerted at the thought that yet another empire that " rules the waves " even in our own day might follow

[13] *Ibid.*, 46.
[14] *Ibid.*, 254.

its predecessors in decline.[15] Now a preoccupation with decay such as underlies Toynbee's work need not in itself vitiate study of the birth of civilization; however, the " change and identity " of cultural forms must not be handled mechanically but with all the reverence for the singular which historical material demands. And it is here rather than in errors of fact (which are inevitable in a work of this scope) that we find Toynbee's work defective. We must, moreover, take exception to his lack of critical precision and to the inadequacy of his conceptual apparatus.

Toynbee, like Spengler, invests certain images which he uses with a spurious reality. These ostensible similes pervade the argument with an implied assurance that they reflect historical situations. When Toynbee compares civilizations with motor cars on a one-way street,[16] or with men resting or climbing on a mountainside, he conveys the impression (which he himself judges correct) that a definite direction, a forward or upward movement, is discernible in history. But such dynamics are imputed, not observed. He writes:

Primitive societies, as we know them by direct observation, may be likened to people lying torpid upon a ledge on a mountainside, with a precipice below and a precipice above; civilizations may be likened to companions of these " sleepers of Ephesus " who have just risen to their feet and have started to climb on up the face of the cliff.[17]

This image (further elaborated in the book, and duly illustrated with a picture in *Time* magazine) does a great deal more than tell us that primitive societies are static and civilizations dynamic. The dominating feature of the image is the rock cliff with its succession of ledges and precipices. Where is the historical reality

[15] *Horizon*, Vol. XV, No. 85 (London, January 1947), 25–6.
[16] *A Study of History*, I, 176.
[17] *Op. cit.*, I, 193.

corresponding to this scenery which exists *independent* of the sleepers and climbers and *determines* their direction? The "one-way street" likewise suggests a predetermined orientation and limitation of cultural endeavour. Toynbee believes that there is a cliff to be climbed, a street to be followed. Yet the truth is—in the terms of his images—that we see figures at rest or on the move in a cloudy space but know nothing about their relative position: we do not know which ledge is above or below which other ledge. Or again: we see motor cars moving, halting, or out of order. But we do not know whether they move in an alley, or on a four-drive highway, on an open plain, or within a circle— we do not even know whether there is an entrance or exit at all.

Toynbee's images betray an evolutionistic as well as a moral bias which interferes with the historian's supreme duty of doing justice to each civilization on its own terms. Why should we characterize civilizations which have achieved a deep and lasting harmony (like those of the Zuni or of certain Polynesians) as " arrested civilizations " where " no energy is left over for reconnoitring the course of the road ahead, or the face of the cliff above them, with a view to a further advance "?[18] Where is this road or this cliff? Why should these chimaeras and a feverish desire for " advancement " disturb the satisfaction of people who have attained the double integration of individual and society and of society and nature? Toynbee merely projects postulates which fulfil an emotional need in the West into human groups whose values lie elsewhere. In our own terms: Toynbee declares the " dynamism " of western civilization to be universally valid; and he can do that only by ignoring the " form " of non-western civilizations. But understanding is thereby precluded.

[18] *Op. cit.*, IV, 130.

Toynbee is not the first historian to introduce the notion of "progress" in his work, and the fallacy of this procedure has been well demonstrated by Collingwood.[19] Of his arguments we can quote only two passages. He maintains that a historian comparing two historical periods or ways of life must be able to "understand (them) historically, that is with enough sympathy and insight to reconstruct their experience for himself." But that means that he has already accepted them as things to be judged by their own standards. Each is for the historian "a form of life having its own problems, to be judged by its success in solving those problems and no others. Nor is he assuming that the two different ways of life were attempts to do one and the same thing and asking whether the second did it better than the first. Bach was not trying to write like Beethoven and failing; Athens was not a relatively unsuccessful attempt to produce Rome."

Collingwood then indicates the exceptional (and really purely academic) case in which one may be entitled to speak of progress,[20] and in doing so touches upon a subject with which modern man is particularly concerned:

Can we speak of progress in happiness or comfort or satisfaction? Obviously not. . . . The problem of being

[19] R. G. Collingwood, *The Idea of History* (Oxford, 1946), 328–30, especially 328–9. The whole section should be read, since our quotations give but an inadequate impression of its cogency.

[20] R. G. Collingwood, *The Idea of History* (Oxford, 1946), 328–30, especially 328–9. "There is only one genuine meaning for this question. If thought in its first phase, after solving the initial problems of that phase, is then, through solving these, brought up against others which defeat it; and if the second solves these further problems without losing its hold on the solution of the first, so that there is gain without any corresponding loss, then there is progress. And there can be progress on no other terms. If there is any loss, the problem of setting loss against gain is insoluble."

comfortable in a medieval cottage is so different from the problem of being comfortable in a modern slum that there is no comparing them; the happiness of a peasant is not contained in the happiness of a millionaire.

Toynbee, though he is less precise than Collingwood, does formulate what he means by progress. He equates it with growth, and " growth is progress towards self-determination."[21] But Toynbee, who is a believing Christian, surely knows that self-determination may not be a matter of gradual advance at all, but rather a flash-like illumination in which one's true nature stands revealed. As a rule, the sequel to this experience is a life-long struggle for a realization of the vision. Why could not this type of self-determination also, like the slow and gradual realization, have an analogy in the life of civilizations? Flinders Petrie and others have maintained that every significant trait of Egyptian culture had been evolved before the end of the Third Dynasty. We find once more that Toynbee has uncritically proclaimed the universal validity of one of several possible sequences. And if he describes " the consummation of human history " as " accomplishing the transformation of Sub-Man through Man into Super-Man "[22] and calls this " the goal towards which ' the whole creation groaneth and travaileth ' (Romans viii, 22),"[23] we may respect his faith but can hardly accept it as the argument of an " empirical student of history."[24]

It is, in fact, odd that Toynbee, who opens his work with an excellent statement of the relativity of historical thought, who complains that " a local and temporary standpoint has given our historians a false per-

[21] A Study of History, III, 216.

[22] Op. cit., I, 159.

[23] Op. cit., III, 381.

[24] Ibid. et passim.

spective," remains himself so completely under the spell of a nineteenth-century western outlook. His evolutionary bias, his empiricism, and his treatment of civilizations as "specimens of a species" are all of a piece. He sometimes equals Spengler in myth-making, treating his equation of civilizations and living beings as a reality, and appealing to biological opinion to uphold a historical conclusion.[25] His use of "species" and "genus" obscures the fundamental fact that science can study individuals as members of a species only by ignoring their individual characteristics. The historian, following this course, would defeat the very purpose of his work.

In fact, Toynbee's vaunted empiricism is an attempt to transpose the method of the natural sciences, where experiment is essential and experience is reduced to figures, to history, where experiment is impossible and experience subjective. Toynbee's "experience" (a word which, in the case of a historian, may stand for intimate acquaintance with historical data) is confined to classical antiquity and its western descendant. It is an odd fact that he should have supposed this limited field capable of supplying the conceptual apparatus with which every historical phenomenon could be comprehended, and that he should have done this, not

[25] Op. cit., I, 172-3. Edgar Wind, "Some Points of Contact Between History and Natural Science," in Philosophy and History, Essays Presented to Ernst Cassirer (Oxford, 1936), 255-64, shows that the latest developments of science, which make it so much less "exact," lead to the raising of questions by scientists "that historians like to look upon as their own." But if these latest developments have made science more "humanistic," Wind is over-optimistic when he says that "the notion of a description of nature which indiscriminately subjects men and their fates like rocks and stones to its 'unalterable law' survives only as a nightmare of certain historians." For many of them (not to mention sociologists) it seems still to be a cherished ideal.

unconsciously, but knowingly, although unaware of the enormity of his assumption. For anyone moving outside western tradition should soon discover the truth that the values found in different civilizations are incommensurate. And so we find Toynbee, like Spengler, doing violence to the evidence and forcing each civilization into a preconceived system of categories. In his case the system is not, like Spengler's, an imaginative construction; but it is derived from the crucial period in western history when the Roman Empire disintegrated. His generalization of particular circumstances results not in historical errors but in irrelevancies. It would be a tedious and laborious task to demonstrate this to the full; but let us take two characteristic quotations referring to Egypt.

Toynbee expects to find in every civilization an analogy of the early Christian Church in the Roman Empire, and thus postulates for Egypt an " Osireian Church " as a " universal church created by an internal proletariat."[26] Now, a " church " as an organized body of believers was not known in Egypt at any time (nor in Mesopotamia, for that matter). The worship of Osiris, always a main concern of the king, spread through all classes of the population, but merely as one among many devotions which filled the life of every Egyptian; the god was never honoured by one group more than by another. And, in fact, no section of the population of Egypt can be called a proletariat if this word is to remain applicable to imperial Rome or to modern times. If, elsewhere,[27] Toynbee describes the expulsion of the Hyksos invaders from Egypt as due to a " *union sacrée* between the dominant minority of the Egyptiac society and its internal proletariat against the external proletariat as represented by the Hyksos "

[26] A Study of History, e.g., I, 143.
[27] Op. cit. V, 28.

one can only say that the words, severally and in conjunction, do not apply. But he continues:

for it was this reconciliation at the eleventh hour that prolonged the existence of the Egyptiac society—in a petrified state of life-in-death—for two thousand years beyond the date when the progress of disintegration would otherwise have reached its natural term in dissolution. And this life-in-death was not merely an unprofitable burden to the moribund Egyptiac society itself; it was also a fatal blight upon the growth of the living Osireian church . . . for this *union sacrée* . . . took the form of an amalgamation of the living worship of Osiris with the dead worship of the official Egyptiac pantheon.

Reading this, one would not suspect that the five centuries following the expulsion of the Hyksos are the most brilliant epoch of Egyptian history. One would also not assume that after about one thousand years of this " life-in-death," religious texts glorifying Amon-Re were written which in profundity of thought and literary splendour belong to the greatest in Egyptian literature, and are its nearest approach to the majestic monotheism of the Old Testament.[28] Surely an " empirical" approach would have started from the fact that Egyptian civilization did actually retain its vitality over an unusually long period. Toynbee, however, declares that the Egyptian achievements in the second and first millennia B.C. are but illusions, for the scheme to which he is committed (although it is alien, and hence irrelevant, to Egyptian history) requires a "time of troubles" before the Middle Kingdom[29]

[28] These texts have been discussed by Kurt Sethe, *Amun und die acht Urgötter von Hermopolis.* " Abhandlungen der Preussischen Akademie der Wissenschaften, Phil.-Hist. Klasse," No. 4. Berlin, 1929.

[29] *A Study of History*, I, 137. It is, perhaps, not unnecessary to add that Toynbee's scheme would be no more relevant to Egyp-

which must be followed by a "universal church" with
its two types of proletariat. Thus the confessed "empiricist" adheres to a preconceived system and disposes of the facts by proclaiming the Hyksos period
"a date when the process of disintegration *would
otherwise* have reached its *natural* term in dissolution." (The italics are mine.)

The scheme which we have criticized in its application to Egypt is intended to render account of the
dynamics of civilizations in their last phases. For the
early phases, the classical world cannot supply ready-made notions. Here Toynbee introduces a set of formulas which may be summarized in his own words:

Growth is achieved, when an individual, or a minority,
or a whole society, replies to a challenge by a response,
which not only answers the particular challenge that has
evoked it, but also exposes the respondent to a fresh challenge which demands a fresh response on his part. And
the process of growth continues, in any given case, so long
as this recurrent movement of disturbance and restoration
and overbalance and renewed disturbance of equilibrium
is maintained.[30]

But communities react differently under a common
challenge; some are apt

to succumb whereas others strike out a successful response
through a creative movement of Withdrawal-and-Return,
while others again, neither succeed in responding along
original lines nor fail to respond altogether, but manage
to survive the crisis by waiting until some creative individual or creative minority has shown the way through,
and then following tamely in the footsteps of the pioneers.

---

tian history if he shifted the date of his "time of troubles" to
the second or even the first millennium B.C. The error is one of
method, not of chronology.

[30] *Op. cit.*, III, 377.

These plausible words do not, upon closer inspection, explain the problem which concerns us. The "creative movement of Withdrawal-and-Return" is illustrated by examples which rob it not only of its obvious, but of all definite, meaning.[31]

The other formula—that of "Challenge-and-Response"[32]—is not evolved from inside history either but is applied, as it were, from the outside; and its applicability, let alone its power to explain the facts, is often more than doubtful. "Challenge-and-Response" is sometimes used to describe a true conflict; sometimes it refers merely to the ordinary seesaw of

[31] *Op. cit.*, III, 248–377. In the history of individuals Toynbee applies it not only to the Buddha or to saints who of their own free will withdrew from society in order to clarify their mission and the message which they were to preach, but also to men like Thucydides, Dante, and Macchiavelli, who were exiled, and bitterly lamented their banishment even though it did not destroy their powers to create. They worked in a solitude not of their choosing and never returned at all, however effective their work may have proved to be in the course of time. Toynbee also applies the formula of "Withdrawal-and-Return" to social groups in a manner which fails to explain anything, as, for instance, when he states that the Nonconformists, after the Restoration, reacted on persecutions by "withdrawing into the realm of private business in order to return omnipotent, a century and a half later, as the authors of the Industrial Revolution" (*Ibid.*, 334). Thus, the interplay of dire necessity and circumstances of every description is reduced to a formula which confuses the issue by a teleological implication (withdraw in order to) which in more than one place (*e.g.* in the image of the climbers and the mountainside) turns Toynbee's account of the facts into mythology. I am purposely avoiding a discussion of Toynbee's examples taken from the Near East or Crete, since I should then have to correct his facts and should become a "critic aiming instruments at bits and pieces" (*Horizon*, XV [London, January 1947], 50.) Readers interested in a detailed criticism by an authority on European history (who likewise considers principles rather than isolated errors) are referred to the essay of Professor P. Geyl in *Journal of the History of Ideas*, IX (New York, 1948), 93–124.

[32] Part of Volume I and the whole of Volume II are devoted to its discussion.

historical fortune. Always, however, it has a misleading ring, since *observed facts* are called a response, to a *hypothetical challenge* construed to meet those facts. In Volume II, "The Range of Challenge-and-Response," we find headings like "The Stimulus of Hard Countries," "The Stimulus of New Ground," "The Stimulus of Blows," "The Stimulus of Pressure," "The Stimulus of Penalization," and so on. The primary data of history merely show that certain peoples achieved greatness; Toynbee thinks that the adverse conditions which he enumerates served as stimuli. That may be so. In any case, it does not explain the fact which, above all others, requires explanation, namely, that in some cases these conditions worked as stimuli and in others they did not. I do not find, therefore, that the formula is conducive to understanding; it must in each case invent a challenge to fit a historical reality which it labels response.

Our criticism does not proceed from a positivistic belief in a so-called "scientific" historiography which is supposed first to assemble objective facts which are subsequently interpreted. Our objection here is not against Toynbee's procedure, but against a terminology which obscures what is the starting-point, and what the outcome, of his procedure. And we make the further criticism that he does not actually evolve from each particular historical situation the notion of a particular challenge to which it can be construed as a response; he applies the formula, as I have said, from the outside, and it is therefore doomed to irrelevance. For example: Toynbee considers the descent of the prehistoric Egyptians into the marshy Nile valley as their response to the challenge of the desiccation of North Africa. In their new homeland they faced, in due course, as a further challenge, "the internal articulation of the new-born Egyptiac society" and failed.

The truth is that the Egyptians flourished exceedingly for two thousand years after the Pyramid Age; but Toynbee thinks they failed because he cannot conceive of a "response" in Egyptian terms, but only in those with which he is familiar: secular government, democracy, and the Poor Law.[33] But since neither the rich nor the poor Egyptians took this view of their state, Toynbee's conclusion is irrelevant. It is true that he quotes the tales which dragomans told to late Greek travellers about the oppressive rule of the builders of the pyramids. But the actual folk-tales of Pharaonic Egypt show us that the people took as great a delight in tales of royalty as the public of the Arabian Nights took in the doings of the despot Harun al Rashid. Snefru, whom Toynbee names, is known as one of the most popular rulers in legend. The fact of the matter is that Toynbee should have started from an analysis of the "response." This would not have shown, as Toynbee has it, that "Death laid its icy hand on the life of the growing civilization at the moment when the challenge that was the stimulus of its growth was transferred from the external to the internal field [from the subjugation of nature to the organization of society, H.F.] because in this new situation, the shepherds of the people betrayed their trust."[34] Studied without preconceived ideas the "response" of the Egyptians stands revealed as a vastly different achievement. The ideal of a marvellously integrated society had been formed long before the pyramids were built; it was as nearly realized, when they were built, as any ideal social form can be translated into actuality; and it remained continuously before the eyes of rulers and people alike during subsequent centuries. It was an ideal which ought to thrill a western historian by its

[33] *Op. cit.*, III, 214.

[34] *Op. cit.*, III, 215.

novelty, for it falls entirely outside the experience of Greek or Roman or Modern Man, although it survives, in an attenuated form, in Africa. It represents a harmony between man and the divine which is beyond our boldest dreams, since it was maintained by divine power which had taken charge of the affairs of man in the person of Pharaoh. Society moved in unison with nature. Justice, which was the social aspect of the cosmic order, pervaded the commonwealth. The "trust" which the people put in their "shepherds" was by no means what Toynbee imagines; their trust was that Pharaoh should wield to the full the absolute power to which his divinity entitled him, and which enabled him—as nothing else could—to ensure the well-being of the whole community.

It seems to me that these discussions have cleared the ground for our understanding. Generalizations based on a limited historical experience, and theorizing, however ingeniously conducted, *must* fail to disclose the individual character of any one civilization or of any one series of events. We must concentrate on what Ruth Benedict called the "selected segment of the arc of possible human behaviour," "the characteristic purposes not necessarily shared by other types of society." In our own terms: In studying the birth of a civilization we are concerned with the emergence of its "form."

II. THE PREHISTORY OF
THE ANCIENT NEAR EAST

AT THE END of our last chapter we said that the study
of the birth of a civilization means watching the emergence of its "form." We have also seen that this
"form" is elusive, that it is not a concrete mould, or a
standard which we can apply to our observations to
see whether they conform with it. We have described
it as "a certain consistency in orientation, a cultural
style." Recognizing it amounts to discovering a point
of view from where seemingly unrelated facts acquire
coherence and meaning. Even so the "form" of a
civilization remains intangible; it is implicit in the pre-
occupations and valuations of the people. It imparts to
their achievements—to their arts and institutions, their
literature, their theology—something distinct and final,
something which has its own peculiar perfection.
Therefore a discussion of the emergence of form entails a knowledge of a civilization in its maturity, a
familiarity with its classical expression in every field.
Then it should be possible to work backwards from
better-known to early times until the point is reached
where the familiar phenomena are lost sight of and
where, conversely, their emergence must be postu-
lated.[1]

[1] We have actually adopted this method in *Archeology and
the Sumerian Problem*, SAOC 4 (Chicago, 1932), an example
followed by Anton Moortgat, *Frühe Bildkunst in Sumer* (Leip-

This procedure, however, has a double disadvantage. It obscures development because it moves against the current of time; and it fails to describe, first of all, the conditions under which the civilization took shape—in other words, its prehistoric antecedents. Now I am not prepared to attempt a definition of the distinction between prehistory and history in general terms, for even within the ancient Near East the distinction is problematical.[2] I shall simply use the term "prehistory" to denote the period preceding the emergence of Egyptian and Mesopotamian civilization, and shall discuss first the climatic conditions in the Near East at that time and then the form of society which prevailed before the events with which we are primarily concerned took place.

At present the arable lands of Egypt and Western Asia are embedded in large tracts of desert. But it seems that in the Ice Age the pressure of cold air over Europe compelled the Atlantic rain storms to travel east by a more southerly track so that the whole area from the west coast of Africa to the Persian mountains was a continuous belt of park and grassland. In Algeria and southern Tripolitania hunters of the Old Stone Age engraved images of elephants, buffaloes,

---

zig, 1935); but the latter book suffers from the confusion caused by an inadequate delimitation of the successive periods.

[2] It would be simple enough if we could equate the beginning of history with the introduction of writing, as is often done. The equation holds good for Egypt where the oldest inscriptions refer to the first identifiable events and personalities and thus, as records of battles and royal names, form the earliest raw material of Egyptian history. But in Mesopotamia this is not so; there civilization took shape, and writing appeared, well before historical documents in the narrow sense came into being. We shall see that this difference between Egypt and Mesopotamia was due to the different purposes which writing and art were made to serve; but it illustrates that generalizations about history and prehistory are hazardous even within a limited field.

and giraffes on rocks now surrounded for hundreds of miles by an arid waste where life is utterly impossible. Paleolithic implements have been found on the high desert which flanks the Nile valley, and in Syria, Palestine, and Kurdistan. Carved tools found in Palestine (Fig. 1, A, B) and the engravings from North Africa find close parallels in the splendid engravings and paintings from the caves of southern France and northern Spain.

We want to dwell for a moment on the paleolithic remains in order to insist that even these distant hunters cannot be understood as " part of nature."[3] From paleolithic times onwards, man has been aware of being involved, not only with his kindred, but with superhuman powers. This dual involvement becomes apparent as soon as we find more than the mere bones and implements of man. In France and Spain hunters of the Old Stone Age left us astonishing paintings and engravings depicting the game upon which they were dependent. These works of art are found in the remote depths of caves and could only be reached at mortal risk. Analogies found among modern people still living in the Stone Age allow us to see in the marvellous images of the beasts, the traces of dancing feet on the soil of the caves, the stones marked with linear signs, the figures of masked or dancing men, expressions of a coherent religious conception, proclaiming man's intimate and reciprocal relationship with the animals, and beyond these, with the divine. Such a brief formula is, of course, ludicrously inadequate;[4] for one thing it

[3] So, e.g. J. S. Slotkin, " Reflections on Collingwood's Idea of History," in *Antiquity,* No. 86 (June 1948), 99. Against this misconception see Helmuth Plessner, *Die Stufen des Organischen und der Mensch,* Berlin, 1928.

[4] For a penetrating study of this matter see Gertrude Rachel Levy, *The Gate of Horn, A Study of the Religious Conceptions of the Stone Age and Their Influence upon European Thought,* Faber & Faber (London, 1948).

substitutes articulate concepts for unreflected experience. But we formulate it in order to emphasize that, from the first, man possessed creative imagination, and we have to reckon with this in considering social cohesion. If the earliest men of whom we have knowledge co-operated in order to trap and kill animals far more powerful than themselves, their hunting differed *toto cælo* from the hunting of a pack of wolves. Their art proves that their relation with their game was not a mere matter of killing and devouring, and that their parties were kept together, not merely by common need, but also by imaginative, religious conceptions, made explicit, not in doctrine, but in acts.

The transition from paleolithic to neolithic culture is not yet known; but we do know that a change of climate, which started in the Old Stone Age, continued in the New, and very gradually changed living conditions throughout the Near East. Libya remained rich in vineyards, olive trees, and cattle up to the end of the second millennium B.C.—a fact which may be surmised from records of booty brought back from there: by a Pharaoh of the First Dynasty;[5] by Sahure of the Fifth Dynasty (about 2475 B.C.), who listed 100,000 head of cattle and more than 200,000 each of asses, goats, and sheep;[6] and finally by Ramses III (about 1175 B.C.), who was still able to take away 3600 head of cattle, in addition to horses, asses, sheep, and goats.[7] At the opposite end of the Near East, in south-eastern Iran, Sir Aurel Stein was unable to round up a "minimum of local labour" to investigate the thickly dotted

[5] On the so-called Libyan palette: Capart, *Primitive Art in Egypt*, 236–7, Figs. 175, 176.

[6] L. Borchardt, *Das Grabdenkmal des Konigs Sahure*, II (Leipzig, 1913), 10 and Plate I.

[7] W. F. Edgerton and J. A. Wilson, *Historical Records of Ramses III* (Chicago, 1936), 67 f. Wreszinski, *Atlas zur altaegyptischen Kulturgeschichte*, III, Plate 66.

ruins of ancient settlements.[8] Nevertheless, progressive desiccation marked the period from perhaps 7000 B.C. onwards, turning the plateaux from grassland into steppe and, ultimately, into desert, and making the valleys of the great rivers inhabitable. When meadows and shrub lands began to emerge from the swamps and mudflats along the river courses, man descended from the highlands.

Now the earliest inhabitants of the valleys were in possession of a considerable body of knowledge which the hunters of the Ice Age had lacked. And we do not know how the change from old to new, from the Old Stone Age to the New Stone Age, came about; for nowhere has a series of continuous remains covering the transition been *recognized*. I use this word advisedly, for we shall see in a moment that the change was of such a nature that its earliest consequences may well defy recognition. We know, however, that this change, like the later one with which we are more especially concerned, took place in the Near East.[9]

The outstanding new feature of the neolithic age is agriculture, with emmer wheat (*Triticum dicoccum*) and six-rowed barley (*Hordeum hexastichum*) as the main crops. Now the wild ancestors of these grains survive even to-day in Syria and Palestine. In the same region, in caves on Mount Carmel, were discovered remains of the earliest men who used sickles.[10] This does not prove, of course, that they *cultivated* grain; they may merely have *harvested* grasses which grew wild. The point is of importance since these people— known in archaeological literature as Natufians—be-

[8] Sir Aurel Stein, *An Archaeological Tour in Gedrosia* (Memoirs of the Archaeological Survey of India, No. 43), 34; cf. 6–7.

[9] R. J. & L. Braidwood, in *Antiquity* XXV No. 96 (December 1950), 189–95.

[10] D. A. E. Garrod and D. M. A. Bates, *The Stone Age of Mount Carmel*, Oxford, 1937.

long to the very end of the Old Stone Age. Yet the
Natufians were the initiators, or at least the early prac-
titioners, of a technique of harvesting which survived
in the earliest agricultural settlements of neolithic
times. Their peculiar sickles consisted of a grooved
haft of bone in which short pieces of flint—"teeth"—
were mounted (Fig. 1 A, B).[11] Such sickles are also
found in the oldest settlements in the Fayum (in
Egypt) (Fig. 1 D),[12] at Hassuna in northern Iraq,[13]
and at Sialk near Kashan in Persia (Fig. 1 C).[14] They
date perhaps about 5000 B.C., possibly a thousand
years or more after the Natufians. In Egypt, during the
First Dynasty (about 3100 B.C.), the sickle-haft was
improved by being curved; it was now made of wood
but retained its cutting edge of small flints (Fig. 1
E),[15] and sickles of this type were used as late as the
Twelfth Dynasty (about 2000 B.C.).[16] In Iraq, too,
sickles with curved wooden handles in which flint
teeth were set were used as late as the Second Early
Dynasty period, about 2700 B.C.[17] In Asia Minor and
Europe no trace of the hafts has survived, but the distinctive flint teeth have been found in Anatolia, South

[11] These "teeth" show a peculiar gloss produced by the silica
in the stalks of grasses so that we are certain that they were
used for cutting cereals. (Cecil E. Curwen in *Antiquity*, IV
[1930], 184–6; IX [1935], 62–6.)

[12] G. Caton-Thompson and E. W. Gardner, *The Desert Fayum*
(London, 1934), 45 and Plates XXVI, XXVIII, XXX.

[13] *Journal of Near Eastern Studies*, IV (1945), 269, 274, and
Fig. 37.

[14] R. Girshman, *Fouilles de Sialk*, I (Paris, 1938), 17 ff. and
Plates VII, LIV.

[15] Walter B. Emery, *The Tomb of Hemaka* (Cairo, 1938), 33
and Plate 15.

[16] W. M. Flinders Petrie, *Tools and Weapons* (London, 1917),
46 and Plate LV, 7.

[17] P. Delougaz, *The Temple Oval at Khafajah* (Chicago,
1940), 30–1, Figs. 26, 27.

Russia, on the Danube, and at the western end of the Mediterranean at Almeria. They occur also throughout North Africa. It is clear, then, that the diffusion of agriculture consisted not merely in spreading the knowledge of emmer and barley but in a simultaneous diffusion of the odd and complex harvesting tool, first used, as far as we know, by the Natufians. Radiating from the Near East, the new knowledge spread in widening circles, reaching the shores of the Baltic and the North Sea about 2500 B.C.[18] However, many questions remain at present unanswered. When did men undertake to improve the wild grasses and to produce, by cross-breeding and selection, the vastly more nutritious grains which were known to the earliest farmers of the neolithic period? When, in fact, was the extraordinary first step taken and the satisfaction of immediate needs limited in order to save seeds, store them, safeguard them against insects and rodents, and sow them when the time was propitious? This may have been done by the Natufians, but of this we know nothing. Furthermore, we do not know how far agricultural methods had advanced when they began to be diffused throughout the Old World. In particular we know nothing about the origin of irrigation, which played so large a part in Egypt and Mesopotamia, and which has been repeatedly recognized as a factor greatly furthering social and political cohesion, since it makes each settlement dependent on its neighbours. We must, therefore, consider this invention.

It deserves notice that irrigation can be resorted to by people who do not cultivate but collect wild-growing plants. This is done, for instance, by certain Indians of the Great Basin of Western North America,[19] and

[18] C. F. C. Hawkes, *The Prehistoric Foundations of Europe* (London, 1940), 82–4.

[19] C. Daryll Forde, *Habitat, Economy and Society* (London,

their methods could very well have been followed by the Natufians utilizing the wadi running at the foot of their cliffs. We may admit, then, that irrigation *could* have been one of the features of the original agricultural complex which spread from the Near East; but there are serious arguments to the contrary.

In the first place, the spread of agriculture seems to have been achieved by means of a slow migration of the cultivators. Primitive hoe or garden cultivation (which is still practised) exhausts the soil it uses. It ignores rotation of crops or fallowing; after some years a fresh piece of ground must be cleared and sown. When the neighbourhood has been farmed, the village moves farther into the bush. The smallness of the neolithic settlements and of their cemeteries,[20] and the manner in which they spread into the European continent, suggests this type of slow but continual migration outwards from the centre where agriculture

---

1934), 35: " In Owen's valley several groups took advantage of favourable conditions to irrigate patches of ground. The growth of bulbous plants and grasses is patently more luxuriant wherever abundant water reaches them, and this was achieved artificially by diverting from their narrow channels the snow-fed streams flowing down from the Sierra Nevada. In spring, before the streams rose with snow-melt, a dam of boulders, brushwood and mud was thrown across a creek where it reached the valley floor. . . . Above the dam one or two main ditches, sometimes more than a mile long, were laboriously cut with long poles to lead the river water out on the gently sloping ground over which it was distributed by minor channels. . . . After the harvest the main dam was pulled down. . . . There was, however, no attempt at planting or working the soil, and none of the cultivated plants grown to the south of the Colorado were known."

[20] V. Gordon Childe, *Man Makes Himself*, 109, states that some of these villages, when completely excavated, covered no more than from 1½ to 6½ acres, lodging from eight to ten households. In *The Town Planning Review*, XXI (1950), 6, he states that sixteen to thirty houses was the normal figure of a local group which he estimates at 200 to 400 souls.

was first practised. There is no dependence on irrigation to be observed here.

In the second place, there are African parallels which suggest that the earliest agriculture in the Nile valley and Mesopotamia could also have proceeded without irrigation. The conditions in these river valleys in antiquity resembled closely those found nowadays on the Blue Nile, where semi-Hamitic nomads, the Hadendoa, sow and harvest in the simple manner which we shall now describe. It is possible, therefore, to postulate similar simple methods for the prehistoric Egyptians. Burckhardt renders his observations in the Taka country of Nubia as follows:

About the latter end of June . . . large torrents coming from the South and South-east pour over the country and in the space of a few weeks cover the whole surface with a sheet of water, varying in depth from two to three feet. . . . The waters, on subsiding, leave a thick slime, or mud, upon the surface, similar to that left by the Nile. . . . Immediately after the inundation is imbibed, the Beduins sow the seed upon the alluvial mud, without any previous preparation whatever. The inundation is usually accompanied by heavy downpours. The rains last several weeks longer than the inundation but they are not incessant, falling in heavy showers at short intervals.

The people appear to be ignorant of tillage. They have no regular fields; and the Dhourra, their only grain, is sown among the thorny trees and tents, by dibbling large holes in the ground, into each of which a handful of the seed is thrown. After the harvest is gathered, the peasants return to their pastoral occupations; they seem never to have thought of irrigating the ground for a second crop with the water which might everywhere be found by digging wells. Not less than four-fifths of the ground remains unsown; but as the quantity of Dhourra produced is generally sufficient . . . they never think of making any provisions for increasing it, notwithstanding that, when the inundation is not copious, or only partial (no one remembers it ever failing entirely) they suffer all the misery of want.[21]

This kind of procedure could not, of course, have been invented in Palestine and Syria where rivers with regularly recurring inundations are unknown. However, the same results can be achieved where there are copious spring rains. Newberry says of the Ababdeh (Hamites living between the Nile valley and the Red Sea): "Some of these nomads sow a little barley or millet after a rainstorm, and then pitch their tents for a while till the grain grows, ripens and can be gathered. Then they move on again with their little flocks."[22]

There are, then, many ways in which a temporary abundance of water can be utilized by simple people to produce crops, and it may well be that the systematic distribution of water which marks the agriculture of historical times in Egypt and Mesopotamia did not exist in prehistoric times at all. We shall see that the problem of drainage was at first as important as that of irrigation, or rather more so; in this respect the modern analogies do not hold good.

The uncertainty attached to the earliest phases of agriculture makes it impossible to speculate on the immediate social consequences of the invention of food production. One would expect these to consist in a greater emphasis on local rather than tribal groupings, a limitation of outlook and horizon, a progressive differentiation of separate settlements as a result of their attachment to the soil. But the introduction of agriculture probably did not mean the more or less speedy

[21] John Burckhardt, *Travels in Nubia*, 2nd ed. (London, 1822), 348–50.

[22] Percy E. Newberry, *Egypt as a Field of Anthropological Research*, Smithsonian Institution, Annual Report for 1924 (Washington, 1925), 435–59.

transition to a fully settled life or to a socio-political organization on a large scale.[23] Nor did it mean that all the other ways of finding sustenance were neglected. A " partial exploitation of the environment "[24] is characteristic of modern savages who have become stuck in a backwater, but not of the true primitives of antiquity. The Natufians may have sown a catch crop or gathered wild grasses, but they also hunted deer and speared fish. All the early settlements of the Near East show signs of a many-sided economy, although in all of them agriculture played an important part. In all of them, too, we find stock-breeding; and this is an innovation which we must simply take for granted since its origin and motivation is at present quite obscure.[25] The Natufians did not possess domestic animals.

Other inventions, too, were known throughout the Near East in the earliest settlements of the New Stone Age. Pottery-making is one of them, weaving another. It is hardly to be wondered that we cannot follow the first phases of their existence. If the earliest pots, for instance, were only dried in the sun or lightly baked or were merely clay-lined baskets, they cannot be expected to have survived. And it may be considered

[23] It seems as undesirable, therefore, to speak here of a neolithic " revolution " as it is to refer to our theme as an " urban revolution " (see below, p. 61, n. 10). Both terms, used by V. Gordon Childe, place the changes in parallelism with the " industrial revolution," but the word " revolution " in this phrase is already used figuratively; it does not refer to an event such as the French Revolution or the Russian Revolution, but to a change of conditions. And by extending its use in this sense, an impression of violent, and especially of purposeful change is made which the facts do not suggest.

[24] R. U. Sayce, *Primitive Arts and Crafts* (Cambridge, 1933), 27 ff.

[25] An attractive guess is made by V. Gordon Childe, *Man Makes Himself* (Oxford, 1939), 87–90. For a recent discussion of the problem which accentuates our uncertainties, see André Leroi-Gourhan, *Milieu et techniques* (Paris, 1945), 96–119.

exceptionally fortunate that of early textiles a few scraps have survived for six or seven thousand years.[26] It is likewise only due to the refinements of modern excavation technique that the oldest of the successive settlements of Hassuna, near Mosul (Fig. 2), was recognized as a camp site, consisting of no more than a number of hearths, still containing wood ashes. They were made of "potsherds and pebbles set in a kind of primitive cement" with pottery lying around them.[27] Only in higher levels did adobe walls appear. This single instance in which a very early settlement was recognized explains why others remain unknown.[28] But we know that after (or during) the time of the Natufians these important discoveries were made and diffused among villages stretching from the Nile valley through the Delta and thence in a great arch (Fig. 51) from Jericho in the south, via Byblos and Ras Shamra on the Syrian coast to Mersin in Cilicia; then, through the Amuq plain, east of Antioch, via Carchemish on the Euphrates to Tell Halaf and Chagar Bazar in North Syria to Nineveh and Hassuna near Mosul, and on eastwards, to Sialk near Kashan in central Persia.

Throughout this region we find small self-contained and self-supporting settlements. Some beads, shells, or

[26] E.g. G. Caton-Thompson and E. W. Gardner, *The Desert Fayum* (London, 1934), 46 and Plate XXVIII. Guy Brunton and Gertrude Caton-Thompson, *The Badarian Civilization* (London, 1928), 64 ff. Jacques de Morgan, *Mémoires de la Délégation en Perse*, XIII (Paris, 1912), 163 and Plate XLIII.

[27] Seton Lloyd and Fuad Safar, in *Journal of Near Eastern Studies*, IV (1945), 271.

[28] This point has been emphasized by Robert J. Braidwood in lectures and papers. See *Human Origins, an Introductory General Course in Anthropology, Selected Readings*, Series II, 2nd ed. (Chicago, 1946), 170 ff., 181 ff. See also Linda Braidwood, *ibid.*, 153 ff. The Braidwoods, excavating in 1948 for the Oriental Institute at Jarmo near Sulimanieh, found remains of a settlement perhaps even older than Hassuna. See p. 29, n. 9 above.

other luxuries may have been imported from more or less distant regions by means of hand-to-hand barter. Occasionally a rare raw material, such as obsidian—volcanic glass, flaked and used, like flint, for tools—was obtained regularly from outside. For the rest, one gets an impression of a somewhat stagnant prosperity in which the great new inventions were thoroughly exploited but little changed from generation to generation for a very long time. There are differences in the crafts: flint tools, pot designs (even ceramic techniques), and personal ornaments differ from region to region and even, as in prehistoric Thessaly, from village to village. There are also changes in style in the course of time. But these local and temporal differences must not detain us as we survey the prehistory of the ancient Near East with a view to the subsequent development. For that purpose we can divide the region into three parts: the two great river valleys and the area between, in which the rich plains of North Syria were the most important part. This central area was prosperous, but it remained unprogressive until the second millennium, dependent on the great cultural centres in Egypt and Mesopotamia. For that reason, we shall confine our attention to the river valleys.

Modern Egypt, even if we disregard the aridity of its climate, differs entirely from the land with which we are here concerned. Nowadays the whole of the country is so intensively cultivated that it does not possess sufficient grazing for its cattle, and one sees cows, buffaloes and asses tethered at the desert edge and fed on cultivated crops such as clover. The river is thoroughly controlled. The desert valleys—wadis—are devoid of vegetation except for bushes of camel-thorn. But in prehistoric, as well as in Pharaonic times, Egypt was a land of marshes in which papyrus, sedge, and rushes grew to more than man's height (Fig. 3). The wadis, too, teemed with life; they are best described as park land where as late as the New Kingdom (1400 B.C.) man could hunt Barbary sheep, wild oxen, and asses, and a wide variety of antelopes with their attendant carnivores. It has been pointed out[29] that the methods of hunting prove that different types of landscape could be found here. Sometimes rows of beaters are shown driving the game towards the hunter or into nets, a method possible only in areas which are somewhat thickly wooded. At other times lassos are used, which presuppose pampa-like open spaces with low shrub.

In the valley, the annual flood of the Nile continuously changed the lay of the land. When the water overflowed the river banks the silt, previously kept in suspension by the speed of the swollen current, precipitated. Some of this precipitation raised the river bed, the remainder covered the banks and the area closest to them; towards the edges of the valley there was comparatively little deposit. Thus banks of considerable height were formed, and after some years the weight of water broke through these natural dikes to seek a new course in low-lying parts, some distance away. The old bed turned into swamp, but its banks remained as ridges and hillocks whose height and area were increased by wind-blown dust and silt caught at their edges. Trees took root, and man settled there, sowing his crops and grazing his beasts in the adjoining lowlands, to retire with them to the high ground of the old banks when the river overflowed. During the inundation, fish, wild boar, hippopotamus, and huge flocks of water birds invaded the surrounding fields and supplied an abundance of food throughout the summer.

[29] S. Passarge, *Die Urlandschaft Aegyptens* (Nova Acta Leopoldina, N.F., Vol. IX, No. 58, Halle, 1940), 35.

All traces of these settlements in the valley proper have long since disappeared; they have been not merely silted over but washed away by the changes in the river's course.[30] This explains why we find traces of early settlements only at the edge of the valley, on the spurs of detritus at the foot of the high cliffs. We must imagine the valley, not flat and featureless as it is today, but dotted with hamlets perched on the high banks of former watercourses and surrounded by an ever-changing maze of channels, marsh, and meadow. Even as late as the First Intermediate period, just before 2000 B.C., the populace of a province in Middle Egypt left their homes and hid in swamps in the valley to escape the dangers of civil war and marauding soldiers.[31] And the early predynastic settlements at the valley's edge were built in groves; among the remains of huts and shelters, tree roots of considerable size have been found.[32]

The prehistoric, "predynastic," period of Egypt clearly falls into two parts or stages (Fig. 4). The earliest of these is known in three successive phases called Tasian, Badarian, and Amratian,[33] each a modified development of its predecessor. Together they represent the African substratum of Pharaonic civilization, the material counterpart of the affinities between ancient Egyptian and modern Hamitic languages; of

---

[30] In 1923 an expedition going to Qau el Kabir in Middle Egypt found no trace of a Ptolemaic temple which Champollion, a hundred years earlier, had marked on his maps on the east bank of the Nile; the river had destroyed both the ruins and the village of Qau and subsequently cut a new bed (G. Brunton, *Qau and Badari* [London, 1927], 2–3, Plate I).

[31] Rudolf Anthes, *Die Felseninschriften von Hat Nub* (Leipzig, 1928), 52 ff., 95 ff.

[32] Brunton, *Mostagedda* (London, 1937), 67; Sir Robert Mond and O. H. Myers, *Cemeteries of Armant*, I, 7.

[33] Amratian is called " Early or First Predynastic " or " Naqada I " in the older literature.

the physical resemblances between the ancient Egyptians and the modern Hamites; and of the remarkable similarities in mentality between these two groups which make it possible to understand ancient Egyptian customs and beliefs by reference to modern Hamitic analogies.[34] The second stage of predynastic culture—called Gerzean[35]—is in many ways a continuation of Amratian; in other words, the preponderantly African character remained. But new elements were added, and these point to fairly close relations with the East, with Sinai, and with Palestine. Foreign pottery was imported from that quarter. A new type of Egyptian pottery, implying a change in ceramic technique, was derived from a class of wavy-handled vases which were at home in Palestine. Several new kinds of stone used for vases may have come from Sinai,[36] and the increase in the use of copper points certainly to closer relations with that peninsula. Although flint remained in use and flint-work achieved an unrivalled beauty

[34] Frankfort, *Kingship and the Gods* (Chicago, 1948), 348, n. 4, and Index, Africa, Hamites. Badarian objects have been found, not only in Middle and Upper Egypt (at Badari, Mahasna, Naqada, Armant, and Hierakonpolis—see Brunton in *Antiquity*, III [1929], 461), but in Nubia (Brunton, *The Badarian Civilization* [London, 1928], 40), in the northern provinces of the Sudan (report of the discoveries of Mr. Oliver Myers of Gordon College, Khartoum, in *The Times* [London] of March 31, 1948), in the desert fifty miles west of the Nile in the latitude of Abydos (*Man*, No. 91 [1931]), and again far to the south, four hundred miles west of the Nile in the latitude of Wadi Halfa (*Journal of Egyptian Archaeology*, XXII [1936], 47–8).

[35] Also called " Naqada II " or " Middle Predynastic." Note that " Late Predynastic " or " Semainean " has been proved a chimera. The remains so labelled belong to the Gerzean period, which thus leads right up to the First Dynasty. See Helene J. Kantor, in *Journal of Near Eastern Studies*, III (1944), 110–46. When we use " late Predynastic " we mean the last part of the predynastic period, in other words, late Gerzean.

[36] A. Lucas, in *Journal of Egyptian Archaeology*, XVI (1930), 200 ff.

and refinement, copper was no longer an odd substance used for luxuries but appeared in the form of highly practical objects: harpoons, daggers, axes (one of which weighs 3½ pounds).[37] The language of the country may also have been affected.[38]

The innovations of Gerzean can best be explained as the effect of a permeation of Upper Egypt by people who had affinities with their Asiatic neighbours and derived from them certain features of their culture.[39] We know that in historical times a similar gradual but continuous drift of people from Lower Egypt into Upper Egypt can be observed.[40] During the Gerzean period the country seems to have become more densely populated; and it has been suggested that the reclamation of the marshland was begun.[41] Such work presup-

---

[37] *Nature*, XII (October 1932), 625; Lucas in *Journal of Egyptian Archaeology*, XIII (1927), 162–70; XIV (1928), 97–108.

[38] The Egyptian language has been explained as a common tongue imposed upon a country where several dialects existed, in the same manner as the French of Ile de France became the official French language, and " Hochdeutsch " the vehicle of communication for all Germans. Now this ancient Egyptian language included two recognizable Hamitic strains—one Southern or Ethiopian, the other Western or Berber—and also one Semitic strain (see the studies of Ernst Zyhlarz in *Africa*, IX [London, 1936], 433–52; *Zeitschrift fur Eingeborenensprachen*, XXIII [1932–3], 1 ff; XXV [1934–5], 161 ff.).

[39] It would be possible to assume that the Semitic elements entered through the Wadi Hammamat from the Red Sea, but this leaves the Gerzean innovations unexplained and ignores the arguments put forward by K. Sethe, " Die Aegyptische Ausdrucke für rechts und links und die Hieroglyphenzeichen fur Westen und Osten," in *Nachrichten von der Koniglichen Gesellschaft der Wissenschaften zu Göttingen*, Phil.-Hist. Kl., 1922, 197–242.

[40] It even affected the physical type of the population; see G. M. Morant, " Study of Egyptian Craniology from Prehistoric to Roman Times," in *Biometrika*, XVII (1925), 1–52.

[41] Brunton, *The Badarian Civilization*, 48. The assumption finds strong support in the tradition that Menes, the first king of

poses co-operation between neighbouring groups and organization of men in some numbers. We may assume that this took place, but on a strictly limited scale. For there are no signs of large political units. There are no ruins of great size, no monuments of an exceptional nature; and if it is objected that these may have existed but may not have been discovered yet, we must insist on the significant fact that among the many thousands of predynastic graves which have been found, there is not a single one which by its size or equipment suggests the burial of a great chief.[42] The Gerzean innovation did not change the general character of the country's culture; the remains suggest a prosperous homogeneous population, fully exploiting its rich environment and loosely organized in villages and rural districts. It was in this setting that the efflorescence of Pharaonic civilization occurred.

In Mesopotamia the corresponding change took place in the extreme south, in the marshy plain between the head of the Persian Gulf and the higher ground which stretches north from Samarra and Hit.[43] This older diluvial part of the country had been farmed already for many centuries before the south was inhabited. The northern farmers had passed through three phases which can be distinguished by their material equipment (see chronological table at end of

---

the First Dynasty, reclaimed all the land from Wasta to Cairo before he founded Memphis at the north end of the strip so reclaimed. Such an enterprise presupposes some established skill in work of that nature.

[42] For a criticism of the hypothetical construction of Egyptian prehistory in terms of united Upper and Lower Egyptian kingdoms in conflict with one another, see my *Kingship and the Gods*, Chapter I, 349, n. 6; 350, n. 15; 351, n. 19.

[43] The head of the Persian Gulf was perhaps 125 miles to the north of Basra; or this area may have been a lagoon, separated from the Gulf by the " Bar of Basra."

book).[44] When the third was predominant in the north, men from the Persian plateau entered the southern marshes. Under present conditions it would be inconceivable that highlanders would elect to do so, or even that they would be able to survive there. But in the fifth and fourth millennia B.C. the Iranian plateau had not yet become a salt desert. Many rivers, descending from the surrounding mountains, ended in upland seas without an outlet and ringed by swamps. Even to-day, in eastern Iran, marsh dwellers are found on the shores of the great lake of the river Hamun.[45] Like the Marsh Arabs of southern Iraq, they build boats and huts of reeds, fish and keep water buffaloes and cattle. Similar conditions must have prevailed over much of Persia in the period we are discussing, and immigrants from such regions would be well prepared to face life in the delta of the Euphrates and Tigris.

The pottery made by the earliest settlers of South Mesopotamia shows that they came from Persia. At first they retained the tightly interwoven geometric designs used in their homeland;[46] but left to them-

[44] The oldest of these is marked by various kinds of simple pottery wares (Hassuna ware) decorated with incisions or merely burnished to a high gloss. In addition there were sickles with flint " teeth " and underground silos for grain storage. Sheep, goats, oxen, and asses were kept. In a second stage appears fine painted pottery, called Samarran—an offshoot of a ceramic tradition at home in Persia. It was, in its turn, displaced by another type of pottery called Tell Halaf, which is found from the Gulf of Alexandrette to the region east of Mosul. The archaeological material is fully discussed in Ann Louise Perkins, *The Comparative Archaeology of Early Mesopotamia* (Chicago, 1949).

[45] See the article and photographs of Melvin Hall in *Asia* (New York), February 1939.

[46] This stage of their ceramics had been known from a small site near Erech (A. Nöldeke and others, *Neuner Vorläufiger Bericht. . . . Uruk-Warka*, Berlin, 1938, Plates 36–40), when it was found well represented at Abu Shahrein (Eridu): See *Illustrated London News*, 11 September 1948, p. 305; *Sumer*,

selves they soon adopted an easier flowing, careless decoration (called Al Ubaid) which remained in use for many centuries and represents the Persian tradition in only a very debased form. In many places it is found on virgin soil, which shows that the settlers spread farther through the country of which they had at first occupied only certain localities. At Ur, for instance, detailed observations were made which reveal the conditions in which men lived when the site was first inhabited. The relevant layers show:

a stratum of irregular thickness composed of refuse resulting from human occupation—ashes, disintegrated mud brick, potsherds, etc. This went down almost to sea-level; below it was a belt about one metre thick of mud, grey in colour above, and darkening to black below, much of which was clearly due to the decay of vegetation. In it were potsherds, sporadic above but becoming more numerous lower down and massed thickly at the bottom, all the fragments lying horizontally; they had the appearance of having sunk by their own weight through water into soft mud. At a metre below sea-level came stiff, green clay pierced by sinuous brown stains resulting from the decay of roots; with this all trace of human activity ceased. Evidently this was the bottom of Mesopotamia.[47]

Southern Mesopotamia resembled the Egyptian Delta, rather than the Nile valley where cliffs con-

---

IV (Baghdad, 1948), 115 ff. There is nothing against calling this pottery " Eridu ware " as long as its historical connections are not obscured. It is quite gratuitous to claim that " Al Ubaid people " can no longer be called the earliest settlers in southern Mesopotamia, for the Eridu ware is simply an earlier stage of the Al Ubaid ware. If quibbles about names are disregarded, it remains true that the earliest settlers of the plain descended from Persia; the new ware shows an earlier stage of their ceramics than has hitherto been found in the plain but it was already known from the western edge of the Highland, *e.g.*, Tepe Khazineh near Susa (J. de Morgan, *Mémoires de la Délégation en Perse*, Paris, 1908).

[47] C. Leonard Woolley in *Antiquaries Journal*, X (1930), 335.

strain the meanderings of the river, and old banks and spurs provide high ground. In Mesopotamia the lowest course of Euphrates and Tigris presents, even today, a wilderness of reed forests where the Marsh Arabs lead an amphibious existence (Fig. 6). All traffic is by narrow bituminous skiffs; the people fish and keep some cattle, living in reed huts built on mattresses of bent and trodden-down reed stems. Their dwellings are described as follows:

at one end is a low and narrow aperture which serves as a doorway, window and chimney combined; on the rush-strewn and miry floor sleep men and women, children and buffaloes, in warm proximity . . . the ground of the hut often oozing water at every step.[48]

The chiefs' reed tents are more impressive; they are large tunnels of matting covering a framework of reed bundles which form semicircular arches. Doors and windows are arranged in the mats closing either end. We know that such structures were also used in the fourth millennium B.C., for they are represented, with all the necessary detail, in the earliest renderings of sacred buildings, notably the byres and folds of temple animals (Fig. 5).

But modern savages are but diminished shadows of the true primitives, and the ancient people of the Al Ubaid period exercised a mastery over the marsh to which the modern inhabitants never as much as aspire. Moreover, the people of the Al Ubaid period belonged to the most advanced group of the prehistoric farmers. Copper was used in their homeland for axes and adzes and even for mirrors. Bricks were known there, too; and brick buildings and the waterproofing of reeds with bitumen are certified for the period. It is likely

[48] Fulanain, *The Marsh Arab, Haji Rikkan* (Philadelphia, 1928), 21.

that some reclamation and drainage of marshland was undertaken. In any case, the men of the Al Ubaid period appear from the first as cultivators, and we are free to imagine their fields as shallow islands in the marsh or as reclaimed and diked-in land.

The vitality and power of these earliest settlers is astonishing. Their influence can be traced upstream, where their pottery replaced the Tell Halaf wares completely, even occurring in appreciable quantities in North Syria. Since it has nothing to recommend it as an article of export, we must assume that its makers came with it and settled widely throughout the upper reaches of Tigris and Euphrates. Nevertheless, the Al Ubaid people were simple cultivators like their contemporaries in Egypt and their predecessors in northern Iraq and Syria. This is most clearly shown by their inability to organize trade in order to obtain the copper which they had been accustomed to use in their country of origin. Once settled in Mesopotamia and removed from the sources of the metal, they used a substitute material that was locally available, making axes (Fig. 7a), choppers, and sickles (Fig. 7b) of clay which they fired at so high a temperature that it almost vitrified and thus obtained a useful cutting edge. These implements were, of course, very brittle and were broken by the hundreds. But they could be easily replaced; and the isolated settlements achieved that autarchy which is characteristic of early peasant cultures.

And yet the Al Ubaid period has left us some remains which suggest that certain centres began to be of outstanding importance and that a change in the rural character of the settlements was taking place. At Abu Shahrein in the south,[49] and at Tepe Gawra in

[49] Ancient Eridu. *Illustrated London News*, 31 May, 1947, 11 September, 1948; *Sumer*, III (Baghdad, 1947), 84 ff.; *Orien-

the north, temples were erected. And these not only testify to a co-ordinated effort on a larger scale than we would expect within the scope of a village culture, but show also a number of features which continue in historical times—for instance: the simple oblong shape of the sanctuary, with its altar and offering table; the platforms on which the temples were set; the strengthening buttresses (which developed into a system of piers and recesses, rhythmically articulating the walls). Moreover, it is likely that at Eridu there was continuity, not only of architectural development, but of worship. In the absence of inscriptions this contention cannot be proved. But the god worshipped there in historical times was called Enki—lord of the earth, but also god of the sweet waters. He is depicted surrounded by waters (for he " had founded his chamber in the deep ") and fishes sport in the streams which spring from his shoulders. Now an observation made during the excavation of the Al Ubaid temples suggests that the same god was adored in them. At one stage the offering table and sanctuary were covered with a layer of fish bones six inches deep, remains, no doubt, of an offering to the god of whom it was said:

When Enki rose, the fishes rose and adored him.

He stood, a marvel unto the Apsu (Deep),

Brought joy to the Engur (Deep).

To the sea it seemed that awe was upon him,

To the Great River it seemed that terror hovered around him

While at the same time the south wind stirred the depths of the Euphrates.[50]

---

talia, XVII (Rome, 1948), 115–22. *Sumer,* IV (1948), 115 ff. shows the development from a very small and primitive village shrine in the earliest layer to a building recognizable in its main features as the prototype of later temples.

[50] After T. Jacobsen in *Journal of Near Eastern Studies,* V (1946), 140.

The importance which one attaches to these signs of a possible continuity remains a matter of personal judgment. But, in any case, the Al Ubaid culture which we have described was the first to have occupied Mesopotamia as a whole. It seems to have spread along the rivers from the south.[51] And it was in the south that, after an interval, the profound change was brought about which made first Sumer, and then Babylon, the cultural centre of Western Asia for three thousand years.

[51] We cannot say for certain whether its bearers were the Sumerians who created the earliest civilization of Mesopotamia in the subsequent—the Protoliterate—period. But no decisive proof for a later arrival of the Sumerians has been offered, and the continuity in cult and architecture support the view that they were the dominant element in the Al Ubaid period, as they remained throughout the third millennium in the south of the country. See also p. 51, n. 1 below.

III. THE CITIES OF
MESOPOTAMIA

THE SCENE we have so far surveyed has been somewhat
monotonous. The differences between the various
groups of prehistoric farmers are insignificant beside
the overriding similarity of their mode of life, relatively isolated as they were and almost entirely self-
sufficient in their small villages. But by the middle of
the fourth millennium B.C. this picture changed, first in
Mesopotamia and a little later in Egypt; and the
change may be described in terms of archaeological
evidence. In Mesopotamia we find a considerable increase in the size of settlements and buildings such as
temples. For the first time we can properly speak of
monumental architecture as a dominant feature of siz-
able cities. In Egypt, too, monumental architecture appeared; and in both countries writing was introduced,
new techniques were mastered, and representational
art—as distinct from the mainly decorative art of the
preceding period—made its first appearance.

It is important to realize that the change was not a
quantitative one. If one stresses the increased food
supply or the expansion of human skill and enterprise;
or if one combines both elements by proclaiming irrigation a triumph of skill which produced abundance;
even if one emphasizes the contrast between the cir-
cumscribed existence of the prehistoric villagers and
the richer, more varied, and more complex life in the

cities—one misses the point. All these quantitative evaluations lead to generalizations which obscure the very problem with which we are concerned. For a comparison between Egypt and Mesopotamia discloses, not only that writing, representational art, monumental architecture, and a new kind of political coherence were introduced in the two countries; it also reveals the striking fact that the purpose of their writing, the contents of their representations, the functions of their monumental buildings, and the structure of their new societies differed completely. What we observe is not merely the establishment of civilized life, but the emergence, concretely, of the distinctive "forms" of Egyptian and Mesopotamian civilization.

It is necessary to anticipate here and to substantiate the contrast. The earliest written documents of Mesopotamia served a severely practical purpose; they facilitated the administration of large economic units, the temple communities. The earliest Egyptian inscriptions were legends on royal monuments or seal engravings identifying the king's officials. The earliest representations in Mesopotamian art are preponderantly religious; in Egyptian art they celebrate royal achievements and consist of historical subjects. Monumental architecture consists, in Mesopotamia, of temples, in Egypt of royal tombs. The earliest civilized society of Mesopotamia crystallized in separate nuclei, a number of distinct, autonomous cities—clear-cut, self-assertive polities—with the surrounding lands to sustain each one. Egyptian society assumed the form of the single, united, but rural, domain of an absolute monarch.

The evidence from Egypt, which is the more extensive, indicates the transition was neither slow nor gradual. It is true that towards the end of the prehistoric period certain innovations heralded the coming age. But when the change occurred it had the character of a crisis, affecting every aspect of life at once but passing within the space of a few generations. Then followed—from the middle of the First until the end of the Third Dynasty—a period of consolidation and experiment, and with this the formative phase of Egyptian civilization was concluded. Few things that mattered in Pharaonic Egypt were without roots in that first great age of creativity.

In Mesopotamia a parallel development possessed a somewhat different character. It likewise affected every field of cultural activity at once, but it lacked the finality of its Egyptian counterpart. It cannot be said of Mesopotamia that its civilization evolved in all its significant aspects from the achievements of one short period, decisive as that had been. Mesopotamian history shows a succession of upheavals, at intervals of but a few centuries, which did more than modify its political complexion. For instance, the Sumerian language,[1] which was dominant throughout the formative phase of Mesopotamian civilization, was replaced by

[1] The earliest tablets, of the Protoliterate period, seem to be written in Sumerian. They use the Sumerian sexagesimal system (with units for 10, 60, 600, and 3600) and refer to Sumerian gods like Enlil. But Sumerian has no clearly recognized affinity to other tongues.

It is important to realize that the term "Sumerian," strictly speaking, can be used only for this language. There is no physical type which can be called by that name. From Al Ubaid times until the present day, the population of Mesopotamia has consisted of men predominantly belonging to the Mediterranean or Brown race, with a noticeable admixture of broad-headed mountaineers from the north-east. This is, for instance, true of the Early Dynastic period, as the skulls from Al Ubaid and Kish show. Skeletons of the earliest known inhabitants of the plain, found at Eridu and Hassuna, have been briefly discussed by C. S. Coon in *Sumer*, V (1949), 103–6; VI (1950), 93–6. They represent "rather heavy-boned prognathous and large-toothed mediterraneans." The much-discussed problem of the origin of the Sumerians may well turn out to be the chase of a chimera.

Semitic Akkadian during the second half of the third millennium. And the shift of the centre of power, in the third millennium, from Sumer in the extreme south to Babylonia in the centre, in the second millennium to Assyria, in the extreme north, brought with it important cultural changes. Yet notwithstanding all the changes, Mesopotamian civilization never lost its identity; its " form " was modified by its turbulent history, but it was never destroyed.

We shall now desist from comparisons and consider the formative age of Mesopotamia, which is called the Protoliterate period since it witnessed the invention of writing. To this period the earliest ruins of cities belong. Now one may say that the birth of Mesopotamian civilization, like its subsequent growth, occurred under the sign of the city. To understand the importance of the city as a factor in the shaping of society, one must not think of it as a mere conglomeration of people. Most modern cities have lost the peculiar characteristic of individuality which we can observe in cities of Renaissance Italy, of Medieval Europe, of Greece, and of Mesopotamia. In these countries the physical existence of the city is but an outward sign of close communal affinities which dominate the life of every dweller within the walls. The city sets its citizens apart from the other inhabitants of the land. It determines their relations with the outside world. It produces an intensified self-consciousness in its burghers, to whom the collective achievements are a source of pride. The communal life of prehistoric times became civic life.

The change, however, was not without its disadvantages, especially in a country like Mesopotamia. The modest life of the prehistoric villager had fitted well enough into the natural surroundings, but the city was a questionable institution, at variance, rather than in keeping, with the natural order. This fact was brought home by the frequent floods and storms, droughts and marsh-fires with which the gods destroyed man's work. For in Mesopotamia, in contrast with Egypt, natural conditions did not favour the development of civilization. Sudden changes could bring about conditions beyond man's control.[2] Spring tides in the Persian Gulf may rise to a height of eight to nine feet; prolonged southerly gales may bank up the rivers for as much as two feet or more. Abnormal snowfalls in Armenia, or abnormal rainfall farther to the south, may cause a sudden rise of level in the rivers; a landslide in the narrow gorges of the two Zabs or of the Khabur may first hold up, then suddenly release, an immense volume of water. Any one of these circumstances, or the simultaneous occurrence of two or more of them, may create a flow which the earth embankments in the southern plain are not able to contain. In prehistoric times when primitive farmers sowed a catch crop after the inundation, it was possible to adapt human settlement to the ever-changing distribution of land and water, even though the villages were frequently destroyed. But large permanent towns, dependent upon drainage and irrigation, require unchanging watercourses. This can be achieved only through relentless vigilance and toil; for the quickly running Tigris carries so coarse a silt that canals easily get blocked. Even when cleaned annually, they rise gradually above the plain as a result of precipitation; and the risk that they, or the rivers themselves, may burst through their banks is never excluded. In 1831 the Tigris, rising suddenly, broke its embankment and destroyed 7000 houses in Baghdad in a single night.[3]

---

[2] A. J. Wilson in *Geographical Journal*, LIV (London, 1925), 235 ff.

[3] W. K. Loftus, *Travels and Researches in Chaldaea and*

Small wonder, then, that the boldness of those early people who undertook to found permanent settlements in the shifting plain had its obverse in anxiety; that the self-assertion which the city—its organization, its institutions, citizenship itself—implied was overshadowed by apprehension. The tension between courage and the awareness of man's dependence on superhuman power found a precarious equilibrium in a peculiarly Mesopotamian conception. It was a conception which was elaborated in theology but which likewise informed the practical organization of society: the city was conceived to be ruled by a god.

Theocracy, of course, was not peculiar to Mesopotamia: Egypt, too, was ruled by a god. But this god was incarnate in Pharaoh; and whatever may be paradoxical in a belief in the divinity of kings, it at least leaves no doubt as to the ultimate authority in the state and subjects the people unreservedly to the ruler's command. In Mesopotamia no god was identified with the mortal head of the state. The world of the gods and the world of men were incommensurate. Nevertheless, a god was supposed to own the city and its people. The temple was called the god's house; and it functioned actually as the manor-house on an estate, with the community labouring in its service. We shall describe the organization of the temple community at the end of this chapter. It is necessary first to survey the actual remains of the Protoliterate cities—the earliest cities in Mesopotamia.

In Protoliterate ruins the temples are the most striking feature. We have seen how, in the Al Ubaid period, temples were erected at Eridu in the south and at Tepe

---

Susiana (London, 1857), 7–8. On 17 May 1950 the correspondent of *The Times* reported from Baghdad that " after a break in the Tigris bund . . . about 2000 mud houses have already collapsed."

Gawra in the north. But the edifices of the Protoliterate period at Erech are much more impressive. The temple of the god Anu (Figs. 8, 45) was placed upon an artificial mound forty feet high and covering an area of about 420,000 square feet. It dominated the plain for many miles around. Near its base lay another great shrine, dedicated to the goddess Inanna. Several times changed and rebuilt, it measured, at one stage, 240 by 110 feet; at another it possessed a colonnade in which each column measured 9 feet in diameter (Figs. 9, 10). Each of these, and also the adjoining walls and the sides of the platform supporting them, was covered with a weatherproof " skin " consisting of tens of thousands of clay cones, separately made, baked, and coloured. These formed patterns of lozenges, zigzags, and triangles, and so on, in black and red on a buff ground. The cones were stuck into a thick mud plaster which covered the brickwork. The patterning in colour enlivened a façade already richly articulated by complex systems of buttresses, recesses, and semi-engaged columns, and thus achieved an effect far beyond anything which the exclusive use of mud as building material would suggest as attainable.

The most characteristic feature of Mesopotamian temple architecture was the artificial mound, called a ziggurat or temple tower (Figs. 8, 11), the tower of Babel being the best known, that of Ur the best preserved, example. However, ziggurats were not found in connection with all temples. The Protoliterate temple at Tell Uqair, which has the same plan and even the same dimensions as the contemporary temple on the ziggurat at Erech, stands on a platform only a few metres high.[4] I am inclined to see in this an abbreviated rendering of the ziggurat, but the possibility

[4] " Tell Uqair," by Seton Lloyd and Fuad Safar, in *Journal of Near Eastern Studies*, II (1943), 131–58.

that the two differed in significance cannot be excluded. We cannot explain why some temples should lack ziggurats; but we can understand why so many great shrines were equipped with them, and why the staggering communal effort which their construction entailed was undertaken.

The significance of the ziggurats is revealed by the names which many of them bear, names which identify them as mountains. That of the god Enlil at Nippur, for example, was called "House of the Mountain, Mountain of the Storm, Bond between Heaven and Earth." Now "mountain," as used in Mesopotamia, is a term so heavily charged with religious significance that a simple translation does it as little justice as it would to the word "Cross" in Christian, or the words "West" or "Nun" (Primeval Ocean) in Egyptian, usage.[5] In Mesopotamia the "mountain" is the place where the mysterious potency of the earth, and hence of all natural life, is concentrated. This is perhaps best understood if we look at a rather rough relief of terra cotta (Fig. 12) which was found at Assur in a temple of the second millennium B.C., although similar representations are known on seals of a much earlier date.

[5] It is sometimes said that the Sumerians, descending from a mountainous region, desired to continue the worship of their gods on "High Places" and therefore proceeded to construct them in the plain. The point is why they considered "High Places" appropriate, especially since the gods worshipped there were not sky gods only but also, and predominantly, chthonic gods. Our interpretation takes its starting-point from "the mountain," not as a geographical feature, but as a phenomenon charged with religious meaning. Several current theories have taken one or more aspects of "the mountain" as a religious symbol into account and we do not exclude them, but consider them, on the whole, subsidiary to the primary notion that "the mountain" was seen as the normal setting of divine activity.— The whole material referring to the temple towers, and the various interpretations which have been put forward, are conveniently presented in André Parrot, *Ziggurats et Tour de Babel* (Paris, 1949).

The deity represented is clearly a personification of chthonic forces. His body grows out of a mountain (the scale pattern is the conventional rendering of a mountainside), and the plants grow from the mountainsides as well as from the god's hands. Goats feed on these plants; and water, indispensable to all life, is represented by two minor deities flanking the god. Deities like the main figure on this relief were worshipped in all Mesopotamian cities, although their names differed. Tammuz is the best known of them. As personifications of natural life they were thought to be incapacitated during the Mesopotamian summer, which is a scourge destroying vegetation utterly and exhausting man and beast. The myths express this by saying that the god " dies " or that he is kept captive in the " mountain." From the mountain he comes forth at the New Year when nature revives. Hence, the mountain is also the land of the dead; and when the sun god is depicted rising daily upon the mountains of the East, the scene is not merely a reminder of the geography of the country. The vivifying rain is also brought from the mountain by the weather god. Thus the mountain is essentially the mysterious sphere of activity of the superhuman powers. The Sumerians created the conditions under which communication with the gods became possible when they erected the artificial mountains for their temples.

In doing so they also strengthened their political cohesion. The huge building, raised to establish a bond with the power upon which the city depended, proclaimed not only the ineffable majesty of the gods but also the might of the community which had been capable of such an effort. The great temples were witnesses to piety, but also objects of civic pride. Built to ensure divine protection for the city, they also enhanced the significance of citizenship. Outlasting the generation of their builders, they were true monuments of the cities' greatness.

It is in these temples that we find the first signs of a new invention without which the undertaking of works of this magnitude, or, indeed, of communal organization on a considerable scale, would not have been feasible, that is, writing.[6] From the first it appears in the form of impressions made by a reed on clay tablets. The earliest of the tablets, found in the temple at Erech, were memoranda—aids for the running of the temple as the production centre, warehouse, and workshop of the community. The simplest were no more than tallies with a few numerals. Others bear, besides the numerals, impressions of cylinder seals to identify the parties or witnesses to the transactions recorded. Still others indicate the object of the transaction. For instance, a simple inscription may consist of the entry: so many sheep, so many goats. There even occurs a more complex type, namely, a wage-list with a series of entries—presumably personal names—followed by the indication " beer and bread for one day." There is no reason to assume (as has usually been done) that these earliest tablets represent the last stage of a long development; the script appears from the first as a system of conventional signs—partly arbitrary tokens, partly pictograms—such as might well have been introduced all at once (Fig. 13). We are confronted with a true invention, not with an adaptation of pictorial art.[7]

[6] The basic work on the subject of early Mesopotamian writing is Adam Falkenstein, *Archaische Texte aus Uruk* (Leipzig, 1936).

[7] A few words may be added here about the early development of writing; although true pictograms—images of the objects (Fig. 13)—occur, many of the most common objects are rendered by simpler tokens: either highly abbreviated (and hence conventional) pictures, such as a figure with two curved

As regards the art of the Protoliterate period, the vast majority of the extant works deals with religious matters. Sometimes ritual acts were depicted, sometimes an ornamental pattern was built up of religious symbols; and occasionally it is impossible to be certain whether the one or the other was intended. But the reference is, in all cases, to the gods. Among the sym-

---

lines across one end (No. 4), which represented the horned head of an ox (the sign means "ox"), or, more often, purely arbitrary signs, such as a circle with a cross—the commonest sign of all—meaning "sheep." The system, therefore, is a collection of abstract tokens eked out with pictograms. The range of notions which could be expressed was enlarged by certain combinations. The sign for "woman" combined with that for "mountain" meant "slave-girl," since slaves were foreigners generally brought from Persia. The sign for "sun" could also mean "day" or "white." That for "plough" could mean either the tool or its user, the ploughman. Even so the script was of limited usefulness. It could not render sentences, for it could not indicate grammatical relations. Its signs were ideograms which listed notions; and that was what the script was, first of all, required to do. But even within the Protoliterate period a further step was taken towards writing as the graphic rendering of language. We find that the arrow sign, for instance, was soon regarded, not as a rendering of the notion "arrow," but as a rendering of the sound "ti," which means arrow. For the arrow sign was also used to render the notion "life" which likewise sounded "ti." This shows that the rendering of speech rather than notions had become possible. The development of writing consisted of a series of makeshifts and compromises introduced piecemeal when the shortcomings of the system being used became noticeable. Some signs acquired a variety of sound values. Some were used to clarify the sense of other groups, although they themselves were not pronounced at all. (These are called determinatives.) Thus "ti" when it meant "arrow" (and certain other implements) was accompanied by a sign which by itself read "gish" and meant "wood," but which, used as a determinative, merely indicated that an implement of wood was referred to. Similarly, place-names were accompanied by the sign "ki," meaning "earth," divine names by the star sign, and so on. Nevertheless, the fact that phonetic values became attached to most of the signs made the rendering of grammatical endings, and, in short, of true speech, possible.

bols—on seals[8] and in the mural decoration of temples
—plants and animals, especially those upon which man
depends for his livelihood, were by far the most frequent. These were the emblems of the great goddess
worshipped at Erech and throughout the land. They
occur singly or in combination (for instance an ear of
barley and a bull [Fig. 14; cf. Fig. 44]), the vegetable
kingdom often being represented by rosettes. Friezes
of sheep or cattle covered the walls of the Protoliterate
temples—painted at Uqair, inlaid or carved in stone at
Erech (Figs. 17, 18).[9] Implements used in the cult,
such as stands for offerings, were likewise decorated
with animals, as were also sacred vessels: a trough
(Fig. 5), from which the temple flock was presumably
fed, shows sheep near their fold—a reed structure
(srefe) like those still built by the Marsh Arabs in
southern Iraq (Fig. 6); and the building is crowned
by two curiously bound reed bundles which correspond to the oldest form of the sign with which the
name of the mother-goddess was written. Vases and
seal designs showing the performance of ritual acts
(Figs. 15, 44) are also common. Like the symbols used

[8] From Protoliterate times onwards, officials, and later also
private persons, owned seals with which they could mark merchandise or documents. The shape of these seals was peculiar
and remained characteristic for Mesopotamia until the end of
its independent existence in Hellenistic times. They were small
stone cylinders carrying on their circumference an engraved design which could be impressed on a tablet or on the clay sealing
of a jar or bale of goods. Since the purpose of the seal design
was the making of an individual and recognizable impression,
its engraving at all times challenged the inventiveness of the
Mesopotamian artists, who responded with outstanding success.
(In our illustrations the rolled-out impressions, not the seals
themselves, are shown. But see Figs. 35–9.)

[9] The inlays consisted of terra cotta plaques set in among the
clay cones which covered the walls. The carved figures were
executed in stone and fixed to the wall with copper wire through
loops drilled in their backs (Fig. 18).

in decorative art, these acts point consistently to the worship of deities manifest in nature.

The gods were also symbols of a collective identity. Each city projected its sovereignty into the deity which it conceived as its owner. There seems to be a contradiction here: the nature gods whom the Proto-literate monuments celebrate would seem more suit-able for worship by countrymen and farmers than by townsmen as we know them. But our contrast "town versus country" is misleading.[10] While it is true that the city in Mesopotamia was an outstanding innova-tion of the Protoliterate period, the great divergence between city and countryside, between rural and urban life, is, in the form in which we are familiar with it, a product of the "industrial revolution," and emphasis on this contrast mars our perspective when we view earlier situations.

About 400 B.C. roughly three-quarters of the Athe-nian burghers owned some land in Attica,[11] and as recently as the European Middle Ages our contrast

---

[10] The same applies to the " urban revolution "—a phrase often used to describe the birth of civilization. This term has been introduced by V. Gordon Childe, whose great achievement has been the replacement of period-distinctions, which had only typological significance, by others which suggest socio-economic differences. However, in the later editions of his *Dawn of Euro-pean Civilization*, in *Man Makes Himself*, and in *What Hap-pened in History*, his point of view has assumed a Marxist slant which applies to ancient Near Eastern conditions inappropriate categories. His recent article, " The Urban Revolution," in *The Town Planning Review*, XXI (Liverpool, 1950), 3–17, and his recent L. T. Hobhouse Memorial Lecture, " Social Worlds of Knowledge " (London, 1949), seem to embody, however, a change of viewpoint. As regards the term " urban revolution," it can in no way be applied to Egypt, as we shall see, even if we should accept it, with the qualifications stated in our text, for the transition from prehistory to history in Mesopotamia.

[11] This matter has been studied by Professor Elizabeth Visser in her inaugural lecture " Polis en stad " (Amsterdam, 1947), who quotes Busolt-Swoboda, *Griechische Staatskunde*, II, 920

"urban-rural" was unknown. At that time the city was as distinct a social institution as it has ever been, but it was intimately related with the land. Trevelyan writes:

In the Fourteenth Century the English town was still a rural and agricultural community as well as a centre of industry and commerce . . . outside lay the "townfields," unenclosed by hedges, where each citizen-farmer cultivated his own strips of cornland; and each grazed his cattle and sheep on the common pasture of the town. . . . In 1388 it was laid down by Parliamentary Statute that in harvest-time journeymen and apprentices should be called on to lay aside their crafts and should be compelled "to cut, gather and bring in the corn"; mayors, bailiffs and constables of towns were to see this done.[12]

In Mesopotamia, then, many of the townspeople worked their own fields. And the life of all was regulated by a calendar which harmonized society's progress through the year with the succession of the seasons. A recurring sequence of religious festivals interrupted all business and routine at frequent intervals; several days in each month were set aside for the celebration of the completion by the moon of one of its phases, and of other natural occurrences. The greatest annual event in each city, which might last as long as twelve days, was the New Year's festival, celebrated at the critical point of the farmer's year when nature's vitality was at a low ebb and everything depended upon a turn of the tide. Society, involved to the extent of its very life, could not passively await the outcome

---

and also Zimmern, *The Greek Commonwealth,* 228: " Greek civilization is, in a sense, urban, but its basis is agricultural and the breezes of the open country blow through Parliament and the market place."

[12] G. M. Trevelyan, *English Social History* (London, 1946), 28.

of the conflict between the powers of death and revival. With great emotional intensity it participated by ritual acts in the vicissitudes of the gods in whom were personified the generative forces of nature. The mood of these urban celebrations, as late as Assyrian and Neo-Babylonian times, shows that the main issue was still the maintenance of the bond with nature.

We do not know for what reasons certain of the nature gods became connected with a given city. We only know that the city, as soon as it became recognizable, appears as the property of one god, although other deities were worshipped there as well. The city god was sometimes viewed as an absentee landlord, always difficult of approach and apt to express himself somewhat casually in signs and portents, dreams and omens of dubious meaning. Yet a misunderstanding of the commands thus conveyed was likely to provoke the calamity of divine anger.

It is in keeping with the tenor of Mesopotamian religiosity at all times that the relationship between the city and its divine owner could be conceived only as one of complete dependence.[13] Throughout we meet with the sombre conviction that man is impotently exposed to the impact of a turbulent and unpredictable universe. This feeling was rationalized in theology, which taught that man was created especially to serve the convenience of the gods. In the *Epic of Creation* man was brought into being after Marduk, the creator, had remarked casually:

> Let him be burdened with the toil of the gods that they may freely breathe.

The same view is implied in an older, Sumerian, myth in which Enlil breaks the earth's crust with a pickaxe

[13] We have discussed elsewhere the feeling of anxiety which pervades Mesopotamian religion: *Kingship and the Gods* (Chicago, 1948), 277–81.

so that men may sprout forth like plants. And the other gods surround Enlil and beg him to allot to them serfs from among the Sumerians who are breaking forth from the earth.[14]

The belief that man fulfilled the purpose of his being by serving the gods had very remarkable consequences for the structure of early Sumerian society. Since the citizens projected the sovereignty of their community into their god, they were all equal in his service. In practice this service took the form of a co-operative effort which was minutely organized. The result was a planned society, and the remains of the Protoliterate period show that it existed then, although it is better known from Early Dynastic times.[15]

We must start by distinguishing two interlocking but distinct social institutions. The political unit was the city; the economic-religious unit the temple community. Each temple owned lands which formed the estate of its divine owners. Each citizen belonged to one of the temples, and the whole of a temple community—the officials and priests, herdsmen and fishermen, gardeners, craftsmen, stone cutters, merchants, and even slaves—was referred to as " the people of the god X." Ideally one can imagine one temple community to have formed the original kernel of each city; but whether this situation ever prevailed we do not know, since the Early Dynastic tablets acquaint us

[14] *Journal of Near Eastern Studies*, V (1946), 137.

[15] A. Deimel published and discussed the texts. See his " Die sumerische Tempelwirtschaft zur Zeit Urukaginas und seiner Vorgänger," *Analecta Orientalia*, II (Rome, 1931), 71–113. His pupil, an economist, published a study on which we have largely drawn: Anna Schneider, *Die Sumerische Tempelstadt*, " Plenge staatswissenschaftliche Beitrage," IV (Essen, 1920). The Protoliterate tablets offer a sufficient basis for the view that the organization of Early Dynastic times continued in most respects that which was created at the beginning of Mesopotamian history.

1. Sickles of bone and wood with flint "teeth": A, B, from Carmel, Palestine; C, from Sialk, Persia; D, from Fayum, Egypt; E, from Saqqara, Egypt.

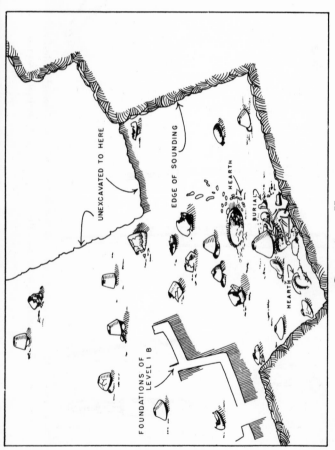

2. Camp site at Hassuna.

3. Papyrus swamp on the Upper Nile. (*Courtesy of American Museum of Natural History, New York*)

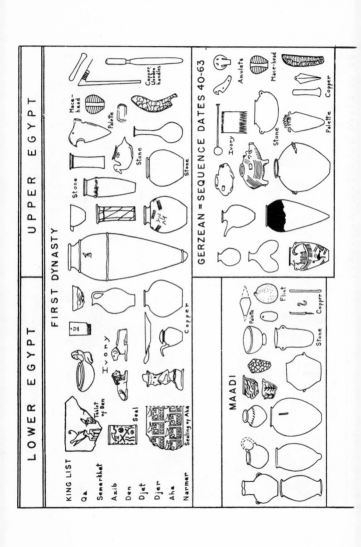

LOWER EGYPT | UPPER EGYPT

FIRST DYNASTY

Stone

Mace-head

Palette

Stone

Stone

Copper Lower handles

KING LIST
Qa
Semerkhet   Toilet of Pen
Azib   Ivory
Den
Djet   Seal
Djer
Aha
Narmer   Sealing of Aha

Copper

GERZEAN = SEQUENCE DATES 40-63

Amulets

Mace-head

Copper

Ivory

Stone

Palette

Palette

MAADI

Palette

Flint

Copper

Stone

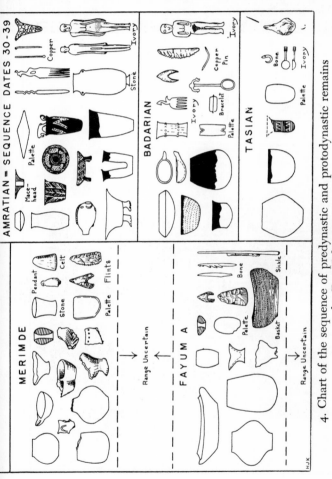

AMRATIAN = SEQUENCE DATES 30-39

MERIMDE

Pendant   Celt

Stone   Palette   Flints

Range Uncertain

FAYUM A

Palette   Bone   Sickle

Basket

Range Uncertain

Copper

Palette   Stone   Ivory

Mace-head

BADARIAN

Ivory   Copper Pin

Palette   Bracelet   Ivory

TASIAN

Bone

Palette   Ivory

4. Chart of the sequence of predynastic and protodynastic remains
by Dr. Helene J. Kantor.

HJK

5. Sculptured trough, Protoliterate Period.

6. Marsh Arabs in Southern Iraq.

7. Clay objects of the Al Ubaid period, from Tell Uqair.

8. The "Hill," "Temple," or "pyramid" viewpoint at Troch

9. Semi-engaged columns covered with cone mosaic, Erech.

10. Colonnade on platform, Erech.

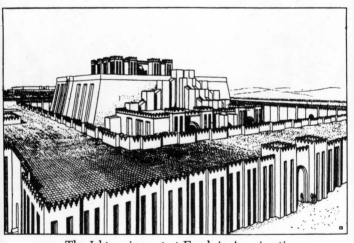

11. The Ishtar ziggurat at Erech in Assyrian times.

12. Fertility god on cult-relief, from Assur.

	A Original pictograph	B Pictograph in position of later cuneiform	C Early Babylonian	D Assyrian	E Original or derived meaning
1					bird
2					fish
3					donkey
4					ox
5					sun day
6					grain
7					orchard
8					to plow to till
9					boomerang to throw to throw down
10					to stand to go

13. The development of Mesopotamian writing.
(arbitrary tokens are not included in column A.—See p. 58f.)

14

15

16

14-16. Seal impressions of the Protoliterate period.

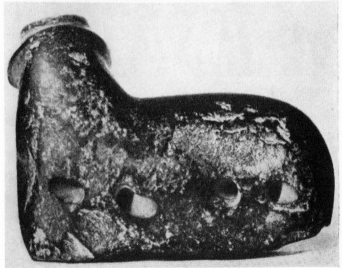

17-18. Stone ram of the Protoliterate period,
Yale Babylonian Collection.

19. Early Dynastic temple at Khafajah.

80. Early Dynastic copper model of a chariot, from Tell Agrab.

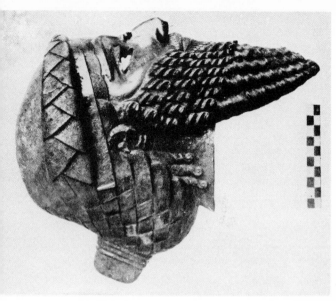

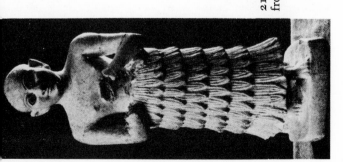

21. Early Dynastic figure,
from Khafajah.

22. Bronze head of an
Akkadian ruler.

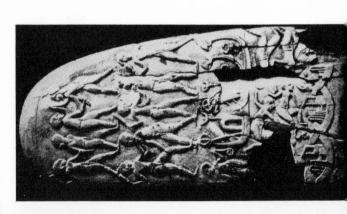

23-24. Knife handle, from Gebel el Arak.

25. The Hunters' palette.

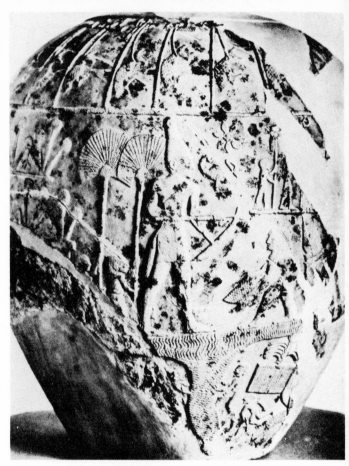

26. Macehead of king "Scorpion."

27. Reverse of King Narmer's palette.

28. Obverse of King Narmer's palette.

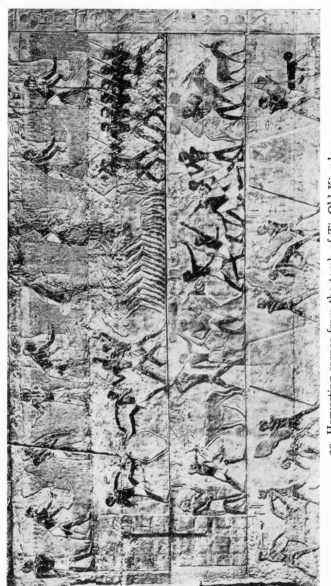

29. Harvesting scenes from the tomb of Ti, Old Kingdom.

30. Agricultural scenes, from the tomb of Menna, New Kingdom.

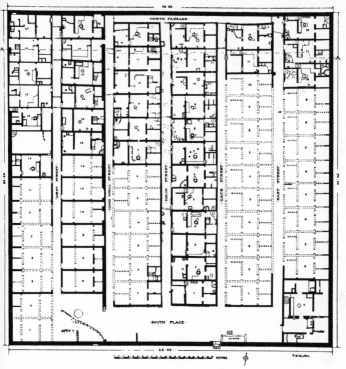

31. Plan of workmen's village at Tell el Amarna.

Impressions of cylinders: 32, found in Egypt, 33 and 34, in Iraq.

25-39. Protodynastic cylinders and impressions from Egypt

40-41. Flint knife with handle of gold-foil, from Gebel el Tarif.

42

42 and 44. Mesopotamian seal impressions (right) and Egyptian First Dynasty buildings (left).

43. Stele of Djet, First Dynasty.

45. "White Temple," Erech.

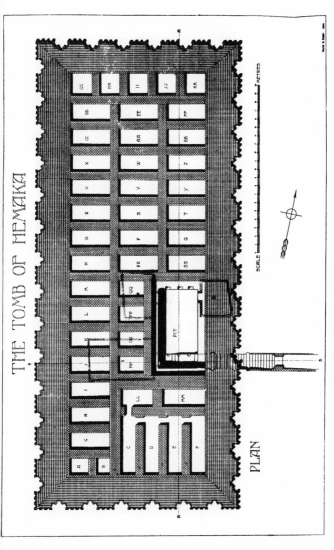

46. Tomb of Hemaka, First Dynasty, Saqqara.

47. Tomb at Abu Roash.

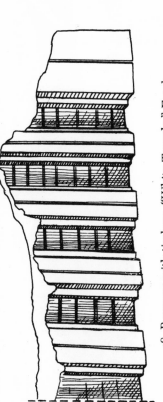

48. Recesses with timbers, "White Temple," Erech.

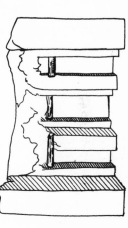

50. Recesses with timbers, Abu Roash.

49. Wooden coffin, Tarkhan.

51. Map of the Ancient Near East, from the *Westminster Historical Atlas of the Bible*. (*Courtesy of The Westminster Press, Philadelphia.*)

with cities comprising several temples with their estates.[16]

Part of the temple land was actually worked by all for all, or again, to put it in the terms of the ancients, by all in the service of the god. This part of the land —not more than one-fourth of the whole in a case we can check—was called *nigenna*-land, a term which may be translated " Common," since the land involved was cultivated by the community as a whole. A second part, called *kur*-land, was divided into allotments which were assigned to members of the community for their support. A third part, called *Uru-lal*-land, was let out to tenants at a rent amounting to from one-third to one-sixth of the yield. Most of this rent could be paid in grain, but a small part had to be paid in silver.

The temple supplied the seed-corn, draft animals, and implements for the cultivation of the Common; and high and low worked every year in the " fields of the god," repairing the dikes and canals as a *corvée*. The *sangu*, or priest, who stood at the head of the temple community assigned the shares in the communal tasks. He appeared as bailiff of the god and was assisted by a *nubanda*, or steward, who supervised labour, magazines, and administration. Stores of grain which had accumulated were not merely used for seed-corn, nor were they exclusively at the disposal of the priest, to be used for sacrifices and for the sustenance of the temple personnel. The priests, like everyone else, had their allotments to support them-

[16] The city god was, for political purposes, and often also as regards the importance of his temple, the chief god of the city. But " the chief god owned only his own temple's land. His relationship to the other gods may most probably be compared to that of the headman of a village to other landowners and their holdings in the village." (Thorkild Jacobsen in *Human Origins, An Introductory General Course in Anthropology, Selected Readings*, Series II (Chicago, 1946), 255.

selves, and the fruits of communal labour returned in part to the citizens in the form of rations of barley and wool, which were distributed regularly, and extra rations, supplied on feast days.

Although the amounts of rations were not equal, nor the tasks assigned to all men equally burdensome, we observe here a fact unparalleled in the ancient world, namely, that in principle all members of the community were equal. All received rations as well as allotments to support themselves; all worked on the Common and on the canals and dikes. There was no leisure class. Likewise there were no native serfs. Some foreigners and prisoners of war were kept as slaves, but private people possessed very few, if any. Slaves worked in the temple alongside free-men as porters and gardeners. Slave girls were kept in considerable numbers as spinners, and they helped in the kitchens, the brewery, and the sties where pigs were fattened.

The allotments differed in size, even when assigned to men of the same profession, and we cannot explain the differences. There is no evidence of large estates in the hands of single members of the temple community, but we may suppose that the existence of several temple communities in one city may have made it possible for some men to dispose of allotments in more than one of them. We know of a *nubanda* who had about 120 acres and a supervisor of the herb magazines who owned about 80 acres.[17] But such conditions represent deviations from the original system. More significant is the fact that even the smallest allotment entered in the temple lists—a *gan*, or seven-eighths of an acre—would suffice to keep a man. Monogamy and the scarcity of slaves would, in any case, limit the area which one family could cultivate.

Women are also listed as holders of allotments, and

[17] Schneider, *op. cit.*, 35.

this means that they served the community in some function or other. For the basic rule of the temple community was that a person received land for his sustenance because he put his specialized skill at the service of all: the shepherd and the fisherman, the carpenter and the smith provided the temple magazines with certain quantities of their produce or simply devoted all their time to work on temple property.

The magazines (Fig. 19)[18] contained an immense variety of articles: grain, sesame seed as the raw material for oil, onions and other vegetables, beer, dates, wine (which was rare), fish (dried or salted), fat, wool, skins, huge quantities of reeds and rushes used for ceilings and for torches, temporary structures, mats for floor coverings and hangings, wood of many kinds, asphalt (used wherever anything had to be waterproof), valuable stones like marble and diorite, to be made into statues and cult objects such as offering-stands, ritual vessels, and the maceheads of the temple guards. The stone, and some of the wood, was imported by merchants, who also brought from Elam aromatics which, in the "oil house," were made into ointments with a base of animal fat. Tools were owned by the temple in great quantities and given out on loan.

All these articles and materials were checked and booked upon arrival and either stored or worked up within the temple precincts. Carpenters made ploughs and other implements, kept them in repair, and built chariots, and probably ships. Tanners prepared skins

[18] The illustration shows a reconstruction, warranted in all essential details, of an Early Dynastic temple excavated at Khafajah by the Iraq Expedition of the Oriental Institute. The magazines were built against the inside of the oval enclosure wall. They surround entirely the platform supporting the shrine and the open space in front of it. See P. Delougaz, *The Temple Oval at Khafajah* (Chicago, 1940).

for harnesses and for leather bottles in which milk and oil were kept. Wool was prepared, and part of it spun, by slave girls; the Baba temple at Lagash employed 127 of these, with 30 of their children. But only 18 were spinners. The others cleaned and prepared the wool, of which large quantities were used in the export trade. A good deal was also distributed as rations to the members of the community. The shearing of the numerous sheep—or rather, the plucking of their wool —was done in a special compound outside the temple precincts, as was, likewise, the milling of the grain.

Barley constituted the main crop, but spelt and emmer wheat were also grown. Monthly rations of barley went from the granaries to the brewery and kitchen of the temple. The brewers also took charge of sheep and cattle to be fattened. But cattle were scarce, for there was little rich meadow land for grazing. The steppe in Iraq will sustain sheep in spring, but the sun burns the grass early in the summer; and even in antiquity the flocks had to be tided over the worst period with grain. In some local calendars there is a month " in which barley is given to the sheep."

The common protein food was fish rather than meat. We have records of private fishponds, and fifty different kinds of fishes are named in the texts. These also distinguish river fishermen, canal fishermen, coast fishermen, and fishermen of the high seas. Sheep and goats were kept for milk and wool. Oxen were used for ploughing, as were also asses. Both oxen and asses were used in teams of four head and fed on barley. The native breeds, deteriorating in the exhausting climate of the plain, were periodically invigorated by crossing with animals imported from Persia. Pigs were kept in the marshes and were also fattened.

Beside extensive cane brakes the temple owned " woods "; these consisted largely of date groves, and there, between the palms, other plants were cultivated, such as grapes, figs, pomegranates, and mulberries.[19] Other groves consisted of timber trees, and there were apple orchards where, it seems, the blind were put to work.[20]

The citizens, when working for the temple, were organized in groups or guilds under their own foremen. These divided the tasks among the members of the group, were responsible for the delivery of the produce, and received the rations for the group. Other lists, enumerating the citizens liable for military service, suggest that the men served guildwise with their foremen as cadre. But there were also professional soldiers, distinguished in two groups, spearmen and shield-bearers. In peace time they worked on the Common, harvested reeds in the cane brakes and assisted in building operations.

The specialization and detailed division of labour of the temple community, and especially the grouping of all kinds of labourers under foremen responsible for deliveries and receipt of rations, offered many opportunities for oppression. But too much can be made of the weaknesses of the system. To speak of the " surplus " of food which must be produced in order to maintain officials as well as merchants and craftsmen, and to imply that the officials must have been a parasitic class which kept the farmers in subjection,[21] leaves out of account several circumstances, of which the most important is the climate of the country. Wherever there is power there is, inevitably, abuse of

[19] *Cambridge Ancient History*, I, 499.

[20] This has been demonstrated by Professor Thorkild Jacobsen in lectures at Chicago.

[21] V. Gordon Childe, *Man Makes Himself*, 152 *et passim*. In *Social Worlds of Knowledge* (London, 1949), 19, he concurs, however, with the view expressed in our text.

power. But the rich soil of Mesopotamia, if well watered, produces food in abundance without excessive or continuous toil. Labour in the fields was largely seasonal. At seed time and harvest time every able-bodied person was no doubt on the land, as was the case in medieval England. But the farmers were not a separate class or caste. Every citizen, whether priest, merchant, or craftsman, was a practical farmer who worked his allotment to support himself and his dependents. Once the seed was sown and the harvest gathered, plenty of time remained in which special skills could be developed, taught, and exploited. There are interesting analogies in villages of our own time, where often enough a farmer or a labourer is a specialist in some branch of craftsmanship. In Europe this condition is rapidly disappearing and was never regularized; but we may quote two modern African instances which will make it easier for us to imagine how practical husbandry and the exercise of crafts and home industry can go together. The modern instances differ, of course, in important details but are instructive nevertheless. It is said about the Nuer:

There are no specialized and hereditary trades though certain persons may acquire a local reputation for skill in making such things as pipes, collars for bulls, canoes or ivory bracelets. These people are not craftsmen by trade, and their activities centre round their cattle, like every other Nuer. Their services are normally accepted by others as part of the integral system of mutual aid which is the basis of every Nuer community, and they are repaid by assistance in pastoral or agricultural activities or by reciprocal gifts.[22]

For another instance, with a rather peculiar character:

In West Africa the Pangwe do not make a business of carving and weaving; all such work is done on the side, in

22 P. P. Howell, in *Man*, No. 144 (1947).

the intervals of fishing and farming. But in so far as a man does carve he is the narrowest of experts. He will manufacture tools but will leave bows to his neighbour, and a spoon carver would never attempt a ladle.[23]

We are reminded of the many names to designate fishermen in Sumerian, even though specialization was certainly less narrow in the Mesopotamian cities. But the point I want to make is that, for all the guilds and professional skills which we find there, the population as a whole was concerned with the primary business of tillage and cannot be compared with any modern body of city dwellers.

Since a considerable proportion of agricultural and other produce passed through the temple magazines, an elaborate system of administration was set up. To illustrate the kind of careful accounts kept of the expenses, we shall quote a record of the grain used in a certain operation. To understand it, it is necessary to know that the fields were ploughed twice, first to break up the ground, then to sow and cover the seed. For the second ploughing a seed funnel was attached to the plough to ensure an even distribution along the furrow. Since the second ploughing was less heavy than the breaking of the ground, the oxen used for it got only half the fodder allotted to the teams used in the first. (The Sumerian measures can be converted by taking the *gan* at just under an acre and the *gur* at about 3⅛ bushels.)

147 *gan* arable land, the oxen put in the plough and seed:

barley for food of the ploughing oxen	24½ *gur*
barley for food of the sowing oxen	12¼ "
seed-corn	12¼ "
waste	1½ "

[23] R. H. Lowie, *Are We Civilized?*, 108.

36 *gan* sown in addition:

seed-corn	3 *gur*
fodder	3 "

Together: 183 *gan* arable land. Its grain Ex-
penditure for the Common[24]   56½ "

This grain came from the temple magazines which had
been filled by the harvest of the Common.

In order to make it possible to draw up a budget,
the yield per acre was estimated, account being taken
of whether the land was good and arable, newly reclaimed, swampy, or distant from water. The monthly
allowances of functionaries were listed, as were the
monthly supplies to brewery, bakery, and kitchen, and
the tasks allotted to the guilds of craftsmen, shepherds,
fishermen; and other specialized workers were also
listed in monthly quotas. All these documents were
signed by the *sangu* and the *nubanda*. But the absence
of money made simplification imperative, since the accounts recorded a continual intake of all kinds of
goods, and the outflow of similarly varied stores, in
the form of rations, sacrifices, materials for repairs,
goods for trade, and so on—which were not reduced to
a common standard of value. It would have been impossible to budget from month to month and from year
to year unless the book-keeping had been adapted to
a somewhat simple scheme with fixed ratios prevailing
throughout. The schematic character of the temple accounts can be seen in the one instance which we
quoted above: the fodder for the sowing oxen was precisely the same quantity as that used for seed. The
span used to break the ground received precisely twice
the amount allotted to the span following after with
the seed funnel. Similar simple ratios were used for
valuations: one *gur* of barley was reckoned equivalent
to one *gin* of silver; one *gur* of barley was likewise

[24] After Anna Schneider, *op. cit.*, 54.

charged as rent for one *gan* of land. It is obvious that such equations reduced the innumerable calculations of the temple book-keeping to manageable proportions. But it is likewise obvious that these simplified and rigid scales never corresponded to the actual values of goods or services. The margin cannot have worked consistently to the detriment of the people, for then the system would have collapsed. Consequently, the margin must have been disadvantageous to the temple economy which could well afford it and which was, in a way, the property of the people as a whole. When in bad years deliveries of certain goods fell short of the quantities due each month to the temple magazines, debts arose and were duly booked and were expected, ultimately, to be paid off. But, on the whole, the organization of the temple economy aimed at simplicity rather than efficiency; and in the Sumerian city, although it was a " planned society," men found considerable scope for private enterprise.

The margin between the schematic values used in dealings with the temple and the actual yield of fields, flocks, and workshops must have given opportunities for some accumulation of private wealth and hence for barter. Craftsmen could utilize their special skills for private commissions as long as they used materials not supplied by the temple magazines. The shepherd could dispose of any increase in his flock beyond the statutory figure; the fisherman could dispose of the remainder of his catch after delivering to the temple his monthly quota. If, therefore, " the people of the god X "—the temple community—can be said to have lived under a system of theocratic socialism, we must add that this planned economy formed a hard core which was surrounded by an ample fringe of private enterprise that remained free.[25]

[25] M. David, " Bemerkungen zur Leidener Keilschriftsamm-

That the accumulation of private wealth was accepted by the community as a matter of course is shown by the rule that a proportion of the rent of *urulal* land had to be paid in silver and not in produce. Moreover, the variety of imported articles testifies to the scope left to barter. It is true that the import and export trade was again organized at the centre. Merchants travelled abroad to obtain stones, gold, silver, copper, lead, wood, and aromatics for the temple. In exchange they could offer grain, dates, onions, and similar produce. But their best opportunities were offered by the produce, not of the rich Mesopotamian soil, but of the skill of the people. Manufactured goods sent abroad included, above all (and at all times), textiles—woollen clothing, hangings, and carpets—and also, to judge by the wide distribution of Sumerian types of tools, weapons, and jewellery, metal objects fashioned in the Plain from imported materials. The merchant in those early days was concerned exclusively with export and import. He did not conduct trade among members of his own community; he exchanged locally finished goods for products of other cities in the Plain or of foreign countries like Elam. It is significant that in return for his effort he received an allotment of land—certain proof that he was in the service of the community. Moreover, he had the use of a team of donkeys belonging to the temple, no doubt in view of his travels (Fig. 20). It seems likely enough that the merchants found opportunities for private trade on the side, and it remains uncertain to what ex-

lung," *Revue de l'Histoire du droit,* XIV, 3–6, has pointed out that the "Staatssozialismus" of early Sumerian times was only fully replaced by a free economy under the First Babylonian Dynasty, about 1800 B.C. Under the Third Dynasty of Ur, private property could consist of houses and the gardens belonging to them, but not of arable fields, which belonged to the temple or to the king.

tent they supplied directly the imported articles found in houses. In excavations, for instance, handmills consisting of flat stones with roundish grinders were found in every house. Yet the hard volcanic stones used for them must all have been imported. In the private tombs of the end of the Protoliterate period lead tumblers and stone vases are common. At Khafajah copper vessels, and stands for stone food dishes, or drinking cups, or lamps, are found in graves of the Second Early Dynastic period. The somewhat later cemeteries at Kish and Ur show even greater luxury and refinement. There were found copper mirrors; copper and gold toilet sets—tweezers, a toothpick, and an earscoop, fastened on a ring and carried in a small conical case; pins of copper or silver with round lapis lazuli heads; beads and animal pendants of alabaster, carnelian, and lapis lazuli, and other semi-precious stones. The silversmith knew how to make filigrain pendants and girdle clasps, and even fine-linked chains.

Most of these articles were, of course, luxuries. In matters of dwelling, food, and clothing, the country was self-supporting. The houses were built of sundried bricks and make an entirely unpretentious impression. They do not show a regular system of planning. Rooms were fitted together as the available plot allowed. Doors were low and arched; one had to stoop to pass from one room to another. Windows were small and high up in the walls and fitted with wooden bars or with screens of baked clay. But the ruins of mud brick do not give a fair impression of the setting in which these people lived. We must imagine the floors covered with smooth, clean rush mats, the walls and benches with gaily coloured rugs and blankets.

The people wore a shawl-like dress, wound round the waist, sometimes with one end pulled round the back and forward over the left shoulder (Fig. 21). It is rendered on the monuments in a manner which suggests sheep or goatskin, but this may be a ceremonial dress only, for it is certain that textiles were worn and they are depicted from the middle of the third millennium onward.

Thus the actual remains found in the excavations demonstrate that the temple community did not impose as rigid a form of life on its members as our description may have suggested; and the texts, in proving the existence of private property and trade, corroborate the elasticity of the system. We know, moreover, that it was able to bear the strain of hard times; for it has been calculated[26] that the temple received a great deal more grain from the *nigenna* land and as rent than was normally needed. The accumulated reserves were made available in an emergency—a better safeguard of the people's food supply than reliance on individual providence might have been. It seems also that the temple supplied rations during the interval between sowing time and harvest, when stores were low.[27]

The accounts of the temple do not differentiate between its role as central store of the community and its religious function; goods withdrawn for sacrifices are treated exactly like those serving for rations. The distinction in function was apparently not made. The temple community was a religious institution regulating the social life of the community, and the two aspects which we distinguish were apparently experienced as one and indivisible.

The temple community seems not, however, to have

[26] Schneider, *op. cit.*, 93 f.

[27] This seems the most probable interpretation of the fact that even holders of allotments received rations during four months. Schneider, *loc. cit.*, 92, views this as payment for *corvée*; but since many holders of allotments, such as craftsmen, worked for the temple all the year round, this seems less likely.

been a political institution. The oldest such institutions of which traces have yet been recognized[28] show the same equalitarian spirit as the organization of the religious community. Political authority seems originally to have rested with the citizens; sovereign power under the city god lay in an assembly—presumably consisting of all free males—guided by a group of elders who seem, moreover, to have been in charge of current affairs. Since the terms for "assembly" and "elders" occur already in the Protoliterate tablets, we can surmise that these peculiar political institutions existed as long as the cities themselves.

It is well to recognize the extraordinary character of this urban form of political organization. It represents in the highest degree the intensified self-consciousness and self-assertion which we recognized as distinctive of the innovations of the Protoliterate period. It is a man-made institution overriding the natural and primordial division of society in families and clans. It asserts that habitat, not kinship, determines one's affinities. The city, moreover, does not recognize outside authority. It may be subjected by a neighbour or a ruler; but its loyalty cannot be won by force, for its sovereignty rests with the assembly of its citizens. Thus, the early Mesopotamian cities resembled those of Greece, of the Hanseatic League, of Renaissance Italy, in many respects. In all these cases we meet local autonomy, the assumption that every citizen is concerned with the common weal, and a small group of influential men who deal with current affairs and sometimes impose an oppressive oligarchy upon the mass of the people.

We do not know whether oligarchic rule ever became a Mesopotamian institution. Our Protoliterate

[28] Thorkild Jacobsen, "Primitive Democracy in Ancient Mesopotamia," *Journal of Near Eastern Studies*, II (1943), 159–72.

sources are too scanty to disclose gradations of power within the existing framework. And in Early Dynastic times, when the texts became plentiful, the framework had collapsed and the old institutions were no more than ghostlike survivals of the past. But it was single rule rather than oligarchy which had supplanted the assembly.

The reason for the change is clear; the equalitarian assembly possessed the disadvantages of freedom to an uncommon degree. Subjection to the will of the majority, as expressed in a vote, was unknown. The assembly continued deliberation under the guidance of the elders until practical unanimity was reached. This might be the result of true agreement, or of mass emotion, or due to a prudent concurrence of the opponents with a line of action advocated by a powerful group. In any case, it was not easily attained; and in an emergency when quick decision and purposeful action was required, the Mesopotamian city, like the Roman republic, put itself into the hands of a dictator. In Sumer he was called *lugal,* which means " great man " and is habitually translated " king."[29]

Kingship was a *bala,* a " reversion," or " return to

[29] The word has not yet been found in Protoliterate texts, a fact which does not prove, of course, that the institution was unknown in that period, although it does make a *prima facie* case for that assumption. On the monuments (Figs. 15, 44) a bearded figure in a long garment is throughout the main actor. He wears his hair wound round his head and gathered in a chignon at the back, a style usual with rulers in the Early Dynastic period. But it should be remembered that the Protoliterate objects on which he appears derive from Erech where, according to the Epic of Gilgamesh, there was a permanent king in very early times. (This was possibly connected with the cult of Inanna.) Note, however, that even Gilgamesh consulted the assembly and the elders before he embarked on a course of action which entailed the risk of war (*Journal of Near Eastern Studies,* II, 166, n. 44). At Erech the ruler was called, not *lugal,* but *en,* " lord."

origin." In other words, the kingly office had a limited tenure; at the end of the emergency authority reverted to the assembly. But, in practice, the threat of an emergency was never absent once the cities flourished and increased in number. Contiguous fields, questions of drainage and irrigation, the safeguarding of supplies by procuring safety of transit—all these might become matters of dispute between neighbouring cities. We can follow through five or six generations a futile and destructive war between Umma and Lagash with a few fields of arable land as the stakes. Under such conditions the kingship seems to have become permanent in certain cities.

Elsewhere the concentrated authority called for by the dangers to which the community was frequently exposed was conferred upon leaders who held important permanent offices. Some of these were exalted enough to enable their holders, when emergencies arose, to exercise power similar to that of the *lugal*. The *sangu* or *nubanda* in the temple of the city god was the administrative leader of the most important temple community in the city. For him to become the political leader of the city was perfectly feasible, but in such a case the official who had usurped the prerogatives of a ruler assumed, instead of the secular title *lugal*, a title emphasizing his dependence on the city god and proclaiming, by implication, the god's agreement with his rule. This title was *ensi*, best translated as " governor " (viz. of the god).

Whether *lugal* or *ensi*, the city ruler in Mesopotamia did not derive his position from any innate superiority or right of birth. He acted either on behalf of the assembly, or as steward of the real sovereign, the city god. In theology, personal rule was sanctioned by a doctrine of divine election which remained the foundation of kingship down to the end of the Assyrian empire. Divine approval could be withdrawn at any time, and the formation of a dynasty, the succession of the son to the throne of the father, although known already in Early Dynastic times, had no basis in the theory of kingship but was interpreted in each case as a sign of favour bestowed by the gods. These limiting conceptions of the monarchy reflect the preponderant influence of the city in Mesopotamian thought. Monarchy remained a problematical institution and failed, therefore, to become an instrument of unity as it did in Egypt. It carried in some degree the taint of usurpation, especially in early times.

The task of the *ensi* in the main was to co-ordinate the temple communities within the city. To each he assigned a share in the common tasks on buildings, canals, and dikes. These *corvées* were then divided among the guilds and individual members of a community by its *sangu* or *nubanda*. The *ensi* dealt, furthermore, with matters of defence and trade, in other words, with foreign affairs. The professional soldiers were under his direct and personal command and formed an important source of his power within the city. Like every other citizen, he received an allotment for his sustenance; but his fields were part of the Common and were cultivated by the people as part of their communal task. Here, again, was an opportunity for abuse of power. Moreover, it became customary to acknowledge the *ensi*'s exalted position by offering him presents on the festivals of the gods. He also took a fee for making legal decisions or decreeing a divorce, and imposed certain taxes. While he administered the main temple of the city, he appointed members of his family to head other temple communities.

Although the assembly seems not to have been superseded entirely, the effective power of the *ensi* was preponderant; and what had been the original strength of Sumerian society, its integration with the temple organization, became its weakness when the leaders of the temple communities utilized the need for leadership, which the growth of the cities called forth, to oppress the people. We know, for instance, that one *ensi* sequestered fields assigned to him on the Common and used them to build up an independent " estate of the palace," modelled on that of the temple. The tablets from Fara show how varied an assortment of people had become directly dependent upon the *ensi*: scribes, chamberlains, heralds, pages, cupbearers, butlers, cooks, musicians, and all kinds of craftsmen.[30] An equalitarian society had been thoroughly transformed, and the power assumed by the ruler was reflected in the presumptions and extortions of his officials. In fact, the Early Dynastic period ends, in Lagash, in an abortive attempt to move against the current and restore the theocratic form of its ideal prototype to Sumerian society. An *ensi*, called Urukagina, states that he " contracted with the god Ningirsu (the city god of Lagash) that he would not deliver up the orphan and the widow to the powerful man."[31] He also put a stop to specific abuses: " he took the ships away from the master of the boatmen; he took the sheep and asses away from the head-herdsman. . . .

[30] The enumeration recalls the so-called " Royal Tombs " of Ur, where, under conditions which are as yet obscure, a courtly society had been buried in all its splendour. The riches discovered in these tombs, which belong to the very end of the Early Dynastic period and appear far removed from the simple co-operative society of the ideal temple community which we have described, recall Homer and Malory rather than Hesiod and Piers Plowman. Since Sidney Smith suggested in 1928 (*Journal of the Royal Asiatic Society* [1928], 849 ff.) that these rich tombs, containing numerous attendants killed when the main occupant was buried, derived from the performance of a " fertility rite," the discussion has continued without leading to a decisive conclusion. See my *Kingship and the Gods*, 400, n. 12.

[31] Translation of Col. xii, 25–6, after Thorkild Jacobsen.

He took away from the heralds the tribute which the *sangus* paid to the palace." These "changes," and many like them, listed in the so-called reform texts, mean that the prerogatives usurped by the foremen and officials were abolished and that these rights were vested once more exclusively in the temple as a vital organ of the community.

Urukagina also ended abuses introduced by his own predecessors; he forbade, to use his own words, "that oxen of the god plough the onion plot of the *ensi*." He lowered the fees for interments and for prayer services. He vindicated the right of the lowly man to his property:

> When a good donkey has been born to a royal soldier (?), and his foreman has said to him, " I will buy it from thee " —if he then lets him buy—he shall say: " Weigh out unto me silver as much as is pleasing to my heart." And if he does not let him buy, the foreman shall not molest him.

It is, of course, possible to suppose that Urukagina, by curbing the power of prominent people, was trying, not only to restore the temple communities to their original purity, but also to win the support of the common people for himself. In any case, factors outside his control interfered with his plans. He was attacked by the ruler of the neighbouring city of Umma and destroyed.

The abuses Urukagina tried to abolish were, in essence, those which vitiate the realization of any political ideal. Weaknesses peculiar to Mesopotamia, however, became clear when serious attempts were made to establish a unified state comprising all the separate cities. This change was attempted by Sargon of Akkad and his successors (Fig. 22).[32] Sargon had

[32] The head is uninscribed but represents in all probability one of the Akkadian kings. The eyes were inlaid with precious materials and had been chiselled out by robbers.

been a high official under a king of Kish, and about 2340 B.C. he founded a city of his own, Akkad. He defeated Lugalzaggesi, the conqueror of Urukagina, and other city rulers who opposed him, until he was paramount throughout the country. Similar successes had been achieved before his time, but they had always been short-lived. And while Sargon's rise to power conformed entirely to the older pattern, a piecemeal subjection of other cities, he struck out a new course in consolidating his position. This time the state survived its founder for several generations. The novelty of his approach may be due to the fact that he represented a northern element in the Mesopotamian population which now became dominant for the first time. This is indicated by the inscriptions: royal inscriptions and many business documents began to be written in the Semitic language which is called Akkadian. This change, in particular, is responsible for the opinion held by some scholars that the rise of Sargon represents a foreign conquest;[33] and it is true that the language points to the middle Euphrates and adjoining territories as its country of origin. But this region had been permeated by Mesopotamian culture for centuries, and people from that quarter cannot be called foreigners in the ordinary sense of the word. Already in Protoliterate times Sumerian civilization had moved northwards along the two rivers, as the Al Ubaid culture (probably also Sumerian) had done in prehistoric times. As Roman influence in barbaric Europe can be traced by means of coins, the influence of Protoliterate Mesopotamia throughout the ancient Near East can be traced by the distinctive cylinder seals of the period.

[33] This view has been refuted by Thorkild Jacobsen, "The Assumed Conflict of Sumerians and Semites in Early Mesopotamian History," *Journal of the American Oriental Society*, LIX (1939), 485–95.

They are found as far to the north as Troy, as far to the south as Upper Egypt, as far to the east as middle, or even north-east Persia.[34] At Brak, on the Khabur in northern Syria, 500 miles north of Erech, has been discovered a temple built on the plan of those in the south, containing similar objects and decorated with cone mosaics.[35] Later, in Early Dynastic times, Ishtar temples at Mari on the Euphrates and at Assur on the Tigris were equipped with statues of Sumerian style, representing men in Sumerian dress.[36] Thus it is obvious that there existed along the two great rivers a cultural continuum within which people could move without creating a disturbance in the fabric of civilization. And the change of language to which we have referred, points to a gradual but continuous drift of people towards the south, as if the cultural influences emanating from Sumer attracted those who had come under its spell. Evidence of this movement is contained in Early Dynastic inscriptions. The thoroughly Sumerianized people of Mari, who had adopted the Sumerian script, inscribed their statues in Akkadian. The same seems to have happened at Khafajah near Baghdad. At Kish, a little farther to the south, the population seems to have been bilingual.[37]

These observations in the field of language are valuable pointers; there may have been other, intangible, differences between the northern and the southern elements in the population of Mesopotamia, differences which would distinguish two strains with distinct cultural traditions. And although the old view that the

[34] Frankfort, *Cylinder Seals*, 227 ff.

[35] M. E. L. Mallowan, " Excavations at Brak and Chagar Bazar," *Iraq*, IX (London, 1947).

[36] Walter Andrae, *Die Archaischen Ischtar Tempel in Assur* (Leipzig, 1922).

[37] *Journal of the American Oriental Society*, LIX (1939), 490.

accession of Sargon of Akkad represents a foreign conquest is untenable, his reign truly marks a new beginning. In the arts a new spirit finds magnificent expression, and in statecraft an entirely new attempt is made
to create a political unity which would comprise the
city states but surpass their scope, and which had no
precedent in the past.[38] The house of Sargon appears
as a succession of rulers consistently claiming kingship
over the whole land; and it is possible that their political ideal was not unrelated with the fact that they
were free, as their predecessors were not, from the
traditional viewpoint which grasped political problems
exclusively in terms of the city. For among most
semitic-speaking people kinship provides the supreme
bond. It is possible that the Akkadian-speaking inhabitants of middle and northern Mesopotamia had
always acknowledged loyalties which went beyond the
city proper. In Sumer there is no sign of the existence
of such loyalties, nor was there a political institution
which over-arched the sovereignty of the separate
cities. But of Sargon a chronicle reports: "He settled
his palace folk for thirty-three miles and reigned over
the people of all lands."[39] The first part of this entry
suggests that Sargon allotted parts of lands of temple
communities to his own followers, thus overriding the
age-old local basis of land rights. No conqueror could
rely on the loyalty of the defeated cities, and it seems
as if Sargon built up a personal following, perhaps exploiting kinship ties in the wide sense of tribal loyalty.
Under his grandson Naramsin, governors of cities
styled themselves " slave of the king."

Sargon also seems to have made a bid for the loyalty

[38] However, Lugalzaggesi, whom Sargon overthrew, had assumed the title of " King of the Land."

[39] L. W. King, *Chronicles concerning Early Babylonian Kings*,
II, 5; Sidney Smith, *Early History of Assyria*, 93.

of the common people. This appears from a change in the formula for oaths.[40] The name of the king could now be invoked alongside the gods. This had a definite practical significance: if an agreement thus sworn to was broken, or if perjury was committed, the king was involved and would make it his business to uphold the right of the injured party. This was of the utmost importance, for the judge had originally been merely an arbitrator, whose main task was the reconciliation or satisfying of both parties. He had had no power to enforce his decisions; and if a man without personal prestige did not have a powerful patron to " overshadow him,"[41] there was little chance of his finding satisfaction in court. The new oath formula put the king in the position of the patron of all who swore by his name; in practice he constituted a court of appeal for the whole land, independent of the cities—a step of the greatest importance in the development of Mesopotamian law and society. Another step towards unification of the country was the introduction of a uniform calendar. Hitherto each city had had its own, with its own month names and festivals. Finally, the existence of a single monarch, who styled himself " King of the Four Quarters of the World," served as a perpetual remainder of the unity of the state.[42]

[40] So F. W. Geers and Thorkild Jacobsen; see Frankfort, *Kingship and the Gods*, 406, n. 35.

[41] Frankfort, *loc. cit.*

[42] The Akkadian rulers were themselves apparently too close to the period of local autonomy to draw up a single king list for the whole land. This was done under Utuhegal (*ca.* 2100 B.C.), the destroyer of the Gutian invaders who had overthrown the rule of Akkad. Utuhegal's " pride in new independence and in the ' kingship ' which had been brought back " led to the compilation of the country-wide list in which the traditional lists of local rulers of the important cities were combined (Thorkild Jacobsen, *The Sumerian King List*, Chicago, 1939). Thus a conception of kingship established by the Sargonid dynasty was projected into the past.

If pressure from the outside world could be relied upon to bring about national unity, Mesopotamia would no doubt have become a single state on the lines laid down by the kings of Akkad. For the country was at all times exposed to great dangers. Civilized and prosperous, but lacking natural boundaries, it tempted mountaineers and steppe dwellers with the possibilities of easy loot. Raids could be dealt with by the cities, but the large-scale invasions, which recurred every few centuries, required a strong central government to be repelled. The safeguarding of the trade routes, too, went beyond the competence of individual cities, and one would expect them to have co-operated in a national effort. Indeed, we find an epic, " The King of Battle," which describes how Sargon of Akkad, at the request of Mesopotamian merchants trading in Anatolia, went there with an army to champion their cause. The story may well reflect an actual occurrence, for Sargon's grandson, Naramsin, built a strong castle at Brak on the Khabur, and the lumber used in its construction included not only poplar and plane, but also ash, elm, oak, and pine, which must have been imported.[43] The Akkadian kings thus undertook a task which occupied all succeeding rulers of the land. Even in the first millennium, the annual sweep of the Assyrian army up into the mountains of Armenia and down towards the west was a sustained and systematic attempt to keep the mountaineers in check; for, with the unlimited possibilities of retreat into their remote valleys, it was impossible to subject them permanently. From Sargon of Akkad on, kings knew that it was necessary to maintain a unified and centralized state; it was necessary to dominate the borderlands sufficiently to meet aggression there; in short, imperialism was the only guarantee of peace.

[43] *Iraq*, IX (1947), 15.

One would expect to find the people rallying to the new order imposed by the Akkadian kings, especially since a feeling of national coherence did exist. The Sumerians had a phrase, "the black-headed people," to designate themselves as an ethnic unit; and the gods Enlil and Anu, among others, were worshipped throughout the land. But this feeling had never found expression in a political form; it remained without effect, it seems, on the country's history. The particularism of the cities was never overcome. At each new accession of a king in Akkad, the land rose in revolt. Far from rallying against the barbarians, the people attempted to revert to the local autonomy which had been the rule before the rise of Sargon. Similar conditions persisted throughout the country's history. For example, the discoveries at Tell Asmar (ancient Eshnunna) illustrate the prevalence of local over national considerations. The ruler of that city collaborated with the Amorites who ravaged the country after the fall of the Third Dynasty of Ur; the barbarians were tolerated, and perhaps even assisted in their attacks on neighbouring towns, which were incorporated into the state of Eshnunna after the Amorites had looted them.[44]

Under the Akkadian kings the tragic pattern of Mesopotamia's history became visible. About 2180 B.C. their dynasty collapsed under the onslaught of the Guti from the Zagros Mountains. Combined invasions of Elamites and Amorites ended the empire of the Third Dynasty of Ur in 2025 B.C. The invasions of Hittites and Kassites ended the empire of Hammurabi's dynasty in 1595 B.C. The invasion of the Medes destroyed the Assyrian empire (611 B.C.). The

[44] H. Frankfort, S. Lloyd, and T. Jacobsen, *The Gimilsin Temple and the Palace of the Rulers at Tell Asmar* (Chicago, 1940), 4, 177–80.

attack of Cyrus the Persian ended Neo-Babylonian rule (539 B.C.).

The absence of safety and stability in the political field is entirely in keeping with the prevailing mood of the country. Mesopotamia achieved her triumphs in an atmosphere of deep disquiet. The spirit pervading her most important writings is one of disbelief in man's ability to achieve lasting happiness. Salvation might be experienced emotionally in the annual festivals of the gods, but was not a postulate of theology.

IV. EGYPT, THE KINGDOM
OF THE TWO LANDS

THE ancient Egyptians said that Menes, who first ruled at This,[1] brought the whole of the land under his control. They designated him as the first king of a first dynasty and thus unequivocally marked the unification of their land as the beginning of their history. If we allow for the telescoping of events by which tradition often credits a single person with the achievements of two or more generations, we may say that archaeological discoveries have corroborated this tradition. The establishment of the single monarchy appears, indeed, as the political aspect of the birth of Egyptian civilization.

We possess contemporary monuments on which two Upper Egyptian kings—" Scorpion "[2] and Narmer—record their conquests in the north country. A votive macehead (Fig. 26) shows the earlier of the two—Scorpion—at the opening of a canal. He wears the tall white crown which in historical times symbolized dominion over Upper Egypt. Above this main scene appear emblems of divinities placed on standards which serve as gallows to *rekhyt* birds; these birds, in all probability, designate inhabitants of Lower Egypt.[3]

---

[1] Near Abydos, in Upper Egypt (Fig. 51).

[2] The name is written with the sign of the scorpion, but we do not know how it was pronounced.

[3] Alexander Scharff, " Archaeologische Beitraege zur Frage

Scorpion seems to have subjected the whole Nile valley, for his monuments have been found as far north as the quarries of Turah, near Cairo.

Narmer, however, extended his power even over the marshlands of the Delta and appears, therefore, as the true prototype of the legendary Menes. Among several monuments of his which have been preserved, a large votive palette of slate (Figs. 27, 28) is the most important. It seems to be a concrete record of the unification of Egypt or, at least, of an important stage in its realization. On one side, Narmer, wearing the crown of Upper Egypt, destroys a chieftain of the northern marshes. On the other side, the king, now wearing the crown of Lower Egypt, inspects a number of beheaded enemies. Thus Narmer is shown as the first "Lord of the Two Lands."

But it would be a mistake to read the Narmer palette as a mere tale of conquest. The "unification of the Two Lands" was, to the Egyptians, not only the beginning of their history, but also the manifestation of a preordained order which extended far beyond the political sphere and bound society and nature in an indestructible harmony. Of this order Pharaoh was the champion. Throughout historical times the texts proclaimed this conviction, and pictorial art expressed it by great compositions in which the towering figure of the king destroys, single-handed, the misguided wretches who have sided with chaos in opposing Phar-

---

der Entstehung der Hieroglyphenschrift," *Sitzungsberichte der Bayerischen Akademie der Wissenschaften, Phil.-Hist. Abt.* (1942), Heft 3, 10, n. 17. Gunn, *Annales du Service des Antiquités de l'Egypte*, XXVI, 177 ff., had seen in the *rekhyt* the people from Lower Egypt. Gardiner, *Ancient Egyptian Onomastica*, I, 100–8, discussed the use of the word at length and hesitated to accept Gunn's conclusion because in later times they are not confined to Lower Egypt; but by then the term, and the use of the lapwing sign, had become purely conventional.

aoh's regimen. It is significant that this aspect of Pharaoh's power should be expressed in art for the first time
in the reign of Narmer.[4]

To appreciate the novelty of the design of the
Narmer palette, we must investigate its antecedents.
Material and shape proclaim it as a specimen of a
common type of toilet article: throughout predynastic
times slate palettes (Fig. 4) had been used for the
grinding of a green powder which, put on the lids,
protected the eyes against glare and infection. On the
Narmer palette, too, a round space is set aside for this
purpose, even though the size of the object seems to
preclude actual use. Now palettes, as well as combs,
knife-handles, and so on, had been embellished with
reliefs during the last phase of the predynastic period.
Among such decorated objects, two treat new subjects.
The first, an ivory knife-handle found at Gebel el Arak
in Upper Egypt (Figs. 23, 24), shows, on one side, the
pursuit of game, a motif which recurs on other objects
of the same age; on the other side is depicted a battle.
The second, the Hunters' palette (Fig. 25), shows two
groups of men who have joined forces in an attempt
to destroy lions, perhaps because these infested wasteland which had to be reclaimed. The two groups are
identified by standards carried in their midst.

The battle scene and the hunting scene are without
parallels in predynastic times. But they are likewise
unconnected with later Egyptian art. Their novelty
consists in the rendering of communal action, their un-
Egyptian character in the manner of that rendering.
Both knife-handle and palette present a faithful record

[4] We confine ourselves to this, the most obvious, aspect of the
Narmer palette as a work of art. But its extraordinary signifi-
cance for the history of art has recently been fully discussed by
H. A. Groenewegen-Frankfort, *Arrest and Movement, An Essay
on Space and Time in the Representational Art of the Ancient
Near East* (London and Chicago, 1951), 20–3.

of the actual course of events: groups of men are engaged in combat or move together towards game. We must suppose that some of the figures stand for leaders or chieftains, but there is nothing by which we can identify them. Each scene shows the melee characteristic of the occasion. But to the Egyptian of historical times such a veristic rendering was totally unacceptable. It hid the true significance of occurrences by merely rendering their outward appearance. However large the masses that moved in battle, built temples or pyramids, went into the deserts to quarry stone or mine gold, they were moved by the will of their divine ruler. Art was adequate to its purpose only if it stressed this fact. It did so by using, throughout two and a half millennia, variants of Narmer's composition. Note that on the macehead of Scorpion, the classical Egyptian viewpoint is not yet rendered in its purity: men are shown to assist the ruler;[5] and the strangled *rekhyt*-birds swing from the standards of the gods. On some other fragments which antedate Narmer[6] the divine standards are provided with hands to show their active participation in a ruler's victory. But on the Narmer palette, as on all monuments of historical times, Pharaoh acts alone. The standards of the gods have become adjuncts to his progress (Fig. 28), and men are merely followers; no act of theirs can be significant beside his own.

If the characteristic Egyptian conception of kingship first received pictorial expression under Narmer, it found its first literary embodiment in a famous text which, from internal evidence, must likewise be as-

---

[5] For the unique features of this scene see H. A. Groenewegen-Frankfort, *op. cit.,* 19.

[6] The so-called Bull and Lion palettes. See Capart, *Primitive Art in Egypt,* 238, Fig. 177; 242, Fig. 181; or Frankfort, *Kingship and the Gods,* Figs. 27 and 28 and 91 ff.

signed to the formative years of Egypt.[7] This is the
so-called Memphite Theology. The lasting value of the
theory of kingship which it expounded is shown by the
fact that the only copy now extant was made as late as
the reign of king Shabaka in the eighth century B.C.
Moreover, it relates the theory with an act of Menes,
the founding of Memphis. The text concerns us, therefore, because of the date of its inception; the act which
it presupposes; and the interpretation which it offers.

The significance of the age of our text is evident. In
view of the overriding importance of the institution of
kingship for Egyptian society, the formulation of a
theory of kingship at the very beginning of the monarchy aptly illustrates the emergence of the "form" of
Egyptian civilization at that critical time.

Reference to the founding of Memphis is made in
our text by implication: its tenor is to emphasize the
profound significance of the city. Thus the content
corroborates the linguistic evidence for an early date
of the document, since a trustworthy tradition, preserved by Herodotus, ascribed the founding of Memphis to Menes. The text expounds the theology of the
new foundation. Of the actual course of events the following account survived into Greek times: it was believed that Menes threw up a dike across the western
part of the valley north of the Fayum, thus compelling
a branch of the Nile to rejoin the main stream, and re-
claiming fifty miles of valley. On the newly won land
he then founded a royal castle, a little to the south of
modern Cairo. It was called "The White Walls," and
thus characterized as an Upper Egyptian foundation—
for white was the colour of the mother-goddess

---

[7] The evidence for the early date is linguistic. Junker's view
on the date of the text is ill-founded. See Frankfort, *op. cit.*,
352, n. 1. In chapter ii of this work English renderings of the
major part of the Memphite Theology are given.

Nekhbet, the protectress of Upper Egypt and of the king's house. But the new settlement was not really a capital of the united country. The successors of Menes in the First and Second dynasties did not even reside there. They seem to have maintained their residence at This and were buried in neighbouring Abydos,[8] within the district whence their ancestors had come. Memphis was originally—and remained for fifteen hundred years almost exclusively (see pp. 97 f.)—a sacred city, the locus where events of unparalleled importance for the Egyptian commonwealth had taken place. The Memphite Theology deals precisely with these events.

We have elsewhere attempted to elucidate the text, which is too abstruse to be discussed here.[9] It translates history into mythology and purports to reveal thereby the transcendent significance of Menes' achievement. Later generations acknowledged the validity of these early teachings by their deeds: each new king came to Memphis to celebrate the " Union of the Two Lands " and to perform the " Circuit of the White Wall," as Menes was thought to have done when he had constructed his royal castle.[10]

The state which Menes created was habitually referred to as " The Two Lands," a designation apt to be misunderstood; we meet here—as so often in Egypt—a term with cosmological rather than political connota-

[8] In recent excavations at Saqqara, W. B. Emery has discovered the tombs of high officials of the kings of the First Dynasty, but there is no evidence, as far as I can see, that there were royal tombs there.

[9] Frankfort, *Kingship and the Gods*, chapter ii.

[10] The reader conversant with the role of Osiris in the Egyptian theory of kingship may here be reminded of the fact that the " Interment of Osiris " was localized in the " Royal Castle " by the Memphite Theology, and that this interment, as well as the resurrection of Osiris in the Djed pillar, was annually performed at Memphis.

tions. We have shown elsewhere[11] that the dualistic mould of the "Kingdom of Upper and Lower Egypt" satisfied the Egyptian mode of thought which conceived totality as an equilibrium of opposites. A meaningful symmetry was imposed upon the unified land, but it had no basis in fact, for Scorpion and Narmer conquered the north piecemeal, as far as we know. Nor is there any sign of resentment against the north. On the contrary, northerners were found among the highest in the land: two queens of the First Dynasty reveal a Delta origin by their names, and officials of that dynasty, buried near their royal masters at Abydos, exemplify the Lower Egyptian physical type.[12]

The outside world did not challenge the exalted view of their state which the Egyptians entertained. None of their neighbours threatened the safety of "The Two Lands"; all of them disposed of natural resources which seemed predestined to be offered as tribute to the divine ruler of Egypt. We have seen that the southern littoral of the Mediterranean was not a desert in antiquity. Narmer's successors had to consolidate their northern frontiers even though they prevailed with ease over the neighbouring populations. Some had to fight the Libyans in the west. At the malachite mines in Sinai, Semerkhet recorded his victory over the local Bedouin on a rock-stela repeating the main motif of Narmer's palette. Another king of the First Dynasty had an ivory gaming piece engraved with the picture of a bound Syrian captive. The roofing beams of the royal tombs at Abydos consist of coniferous wood imported from the Lebanon. Jugs of Syrian and Palestinian manufacture have been found

[11] Frankfort, op. cit., 19–23.
[12] See G. M. Morant, "Study of Egyptian Craniology from Prehistoric to Roman Times." Biometrika, XVII (1925), 1–52.

in these tombs and in those of dignitaries buried at Saqqara: they probably served as containers of olive oil. Gold, ivory, ostrich feathers, and ebony came through Nubia from inner Africa.

However, in this phase of Egyptian civilization, signs of contact with a yet more distant region are also found. They differ in character from those we have just mentioned. Libya, Sinai, and Syria supplied the Nile valley with much-needed raw materials; but Sumer supplied ideas. Imported Mesopotamian cylinder seals have been found in Egypt, and the same odd form of seal was adopted in Egypt. The earliest Egyptian brick buildings resemble the Protoliterate temples of Mesopotamia in all significant matters of technique. Egyptian art—even in the Narmer palette—used Mesopotamian motifs. Even writing seems to have been due to the stimulus derived from acquaintance with Mesopotamian writing of the end of the Protoliterate period.

We have dealt with these matters in an Appendix. For although it is certain that contact between the two great centres of the Near East took place, it did not affect the social and political sphere with which we are concerned here. In fact, if we look back over the evidence presented in this chapter, the autochthonous character of the Egyptian development is unmistakable. The basic structure of the society which emerged was the direct opposite of that which came into being in Mesopotamia. In Egypt the great change did not lead to a concentration of social activity in urban centres. It is true that there were cities in Egypt, but, with the single exception of the capital, these were no more than market towns for the countryside. Paradoxically enough, the capital was less permanent than the towns in the provinces, for in principle it served for only a single reign. Each pharaoh took up residence near the site chosen for his tomb, where, during the best part of his lifetime, the work on the pyramid and its temple continued, while the government functioned in the neighbouring city. But after his death the place was abandoned to the priests and officials who maintained his cult and managed his mortuary estate, unless the new king decided to continue in residence because the adjoining desert offered a suitable site for his own tomb. Until the middle of the second millennium B.C. (when Thebes assumed a metropolitan character) there was no truly permanent capital in Egypt, a situation which clearly demonstrates the insignificant role played by the concept of the city in the political thought of the Egyptians.[13] In Mesopotamia, on the other hand, even the most powerful rulers of the land styled themselves rulers of cities and functioned as such, in Akkad or Ur, in Babylon or in Assur.

The contrast in social structure and the divergent conceptions of kingship can be seen as correlated. The city as the ultimate form of political organization is inconceivable without a ruler who remains potentially one among many; conversely, absolute power entails a unified realm. We did, therefore, not lose sight of our theme when we discussed in this chapter the origin of the myths and rites of kingship under Menes; nor is it due to the accident of discovery that we studied the birth of Egyptian civilization with the aid of royal monuments. For Pharaoh symbolized the community in its temporal and transcendent aspects, and,

---

[13] The rural character of the Egyptian commonwealth became apparent also in times of internal conflict. The wars between the Sumerian city-states find their Egyptian counterpart in struggles in which large parts of the Nile valley appear united under rival chiefs: a Theban family of Antefs and Mentuhoteps leading Upper Egypt against the royal house residing at Herakleopolis; or Kamose or Ahmose leading, first the Thebaid, then the whole Nile valley, against the foreign Hyksos in the Delta.

for the Egyptians, civilized life gravitated around the divine king.

Our discussion of the rise of the monarchical society of Egypt must now be complemented by a concrete description. The administration of the country[14] functioned on the strength of delegated royal power. Pharaoh was the living fount of law, governing by decrees which were formulated as inspired decisions.[15] In early times the government assumed a somewhat patriarchal character. Sons and other close relatives of Pharaoh acted as his principal advisors and aids. Distant relatives and descendants of past rulers were found in minor government posts. At first no single minister stood between the king and the various branches of the administration. There was no Grand Vizier. Under the Fourth Dynasty, however, the vizierate was introduced as the apex of the bureaucracy; but it was, at first, occupied by a prince of royal blood.

Even in later times the king reserved certain prerogatives, such as the imposition of the death penalty and

[14] We may note in passing that the rudiments of the official hierarchy were established in the First Dynasty. Cylinder seals of that period (Figs. 35, 36) bear titles (and presumably names) of officials. The investiture with a cylinder seal confirmed the official in his function, and the term *š'ḥw*, which is usually translated "noble," in reality means "he who owns a seal of office"—in other words, a high official.

[15] This may have been a contributory cause to the extreme scarcity of legal and administrative documents, the main cause being the perishable nature of the Egyptian writing materials— leather and papyrus; but when the king's decision is the source of law, the need of codes and statutes is much reduced (see my *Ancient Egyptian Religion*, 43–6). In any case, the rarity of written documents obliged us to telescope in this chapter evidence much more widely spread through time than we used in our description of Mesopotamia. We have attempted to stress the features of society which we believe to have been present well-nigh from the first and which remained fairly permanent. But we are aware of the danger that we have distorted our sketch of conditions in the early part of the third millennium B.C.

of mutilations; and the vizier had an audience each morning to report on the state of the land. Nevertheless, the vizier's power of initiative was very great. He was Chief Justice, Head of the Archives, and, in fact, of every government department. His messengers travelled through the country carrying his orders to the local administrators and reporting back to him on the conditions they observed. One of his designations was " to whom is reported all that is and is not." In view of the overwhelming importance of agriculture for the state, every transaction involving land had to be registered at the Vizier's office. After the Sixth Dynasty the vizier was, probably for practical reasons, " Mayor of the Town," that is, head and military governor of the royal residence.

The administration which functioned under the vizier was divided into several departments. First among these was the Exchequer, headed by the " Treasurer of the god (*i.e.* king)." This was the central depot for all imposts and duties owed to the state. In view of the ideal form of the Dual Monarchy it was called " The Two White Houses," but in practice there was no division. It had branches with storehouses throughout the country where the dues were collected and from where the central treasury was supplied. The administration was highly centralized; and the Treasurer was responsible, not only for the collection and disposal of the native produce paid in as taxes, but also for the royal expeditions which, as we shall see, brought new materials such as copper, malachite, wood, or gold, from abroad. Therefore he sometimes bore the title " general " or " admiral " and had troops and ships at his disposal.

The second important government department was the Ministry of Agriculture, in which a " Chief of the Fields " dealt with purely agricultural matters, while

a " Master of (the King's) Largesse " was concerned
with everything pertaining to livestock.

These government departments were not rigidly
separated, and an administrative career was likely to
take a man through all of them, as well as through the
local administration. Promising young men, or sons of
those whom the king trusted or favoured, were educated at court, and then acquired administrative experience by passing through a succession of posts
which they filled with the assistance of knowledgeable
scribes of the relevant departments. Methen (Fourth
Dynasty) was a Royal Kinsman who acted successively
as Scribe of the Exchequer, apparently also as Phy-
sician, then as District Chief, Judge, Supervisor of all
the flax of the king, to end as nomarch or ruler of a
province. In this last function he administered three
provinces in succession—which proves that the administration was independent of local worthies. At the end
of the Old Kingdom the nomarchs had achieved some
sort of permanence by regularly obtaining their offices
for their sons as their successors, and so they developed
into a landed gentry. At first, however, they were royal
officials who were moved from one post to another,
who had no pretence to independence and no local
ties. Their affinities and interests—as those of all officials—were with the court; and Methen remained
until the end " Master of the King's Hunt," a purely
courtly function.

Neither the several departments of the government
nor the central and local administrations were clearly
delimited, and their province remained ill-defined until the end. It has been pointed out, for instance,[16]
that, under the New Kingdom, tribute from abroad
could be received upon arrival in Egypt by the
" Treasurer of the god " as head of the Exchequer, by

[16] Kees, *Kulturgeschichte*, 210.

the "Supervisor of the Treasury," his subordinate, by lower officials of the Exchequer, by the vizier, by high military commanders, or by the chief priest of Amon. This fluidity of competence is simply due to the fact that all authority was delegated royal power and hence comprehensive in its very nature. There was similarly a vagueness of demarcation between the central and the local authorities; and when Seti I (Nineteenth Dynasty) issued a decree commanding that the temple of Abydos should receive its shipments of gold from Nubia without being subject to tolls and other dues normally levied from ships in transit, he had to address his decree to twelve different classes of officials, starting with the vizier and so down to "the mayors and the controllers of camps in Upper and Lower Egypt . . . every inspector belonging to the king's estate and every person sent on a mission to Nubia."[17] For local officers, no less than those of the central government, represented Pharaoh. A nomarch of the Fifth Dynasty, Nesutnefer,[18] is marked by his titles as "Leader of the Land (*i.e.* province)," which probably meant that he was the head of the provincial administration in all its branches. He was "Chief of Fortifications," which meant that he was head of the police as well as responsible for the guarding of the frontiers of his province against desert tribes. He was "Ruler of the King's People," namely, of the serfs and tenants, bailiffs and stewards, craftsmen, scribes, fishermen, and so on, who were employed on the royal domains within his province, whether they were free or bond. Finally, he was called "Chief of Commands," which meant that orders from the king or the vizier went to him and that he was responsible for their being carried out in his province.

[17] *Journal of Egyptian Archaeology*, XIII (1927), 200.

[18] Junker, *Giza*, III (Wien, 1938), 172 ff.

In the nomarchs we find an element most dangerous to the unity of the state. Under the Old Kingdom there was, at first, no question of any power opposing the king. Nesutnefer, whose office we have just described, was twice transferred to another province. But the kings rewarded their faithful servants with gifts of land; and, at the same time, officials pressed for hereditary appointments. Officially this claim was never admitted, but in practice there was an advantage in letting a son succeed his father, since the loyalty of the incumbent of an office was then ensured and his successor was certain to receive most careful professional training. However, the two tendencies together changed the relation between the great officials and the king in the course of time. Hereditary offices and property turned the officials into landed proprietors who were no longer entirely dependent upon their function at court,[19] although, as long as the central power remained strong, Pharaoh could cancel all rights to land or to office at any time. Nevertheless, when the central administration collapsed completely at the end of the Sixth Dynasty, the hereditary landowners were in a position to assume responsibility for the maintenance of rule and order in their districts. The manors of their estates were turned into miniature courts. This situation flouted every native theory and practice of government, and it did not outlast the period of confusion. The kings of the Twelfth Dynasty restored centralized government.

It is possible to gain a clear idea of the mentality of the Egyptian official, since many texts define the norms of his behaviour. The ideal official was " the silent

[19] The change was a slow one. Methen (whose career under the Fourth Dynasty we have described) thought it worth while to record in his tomb the possession, not of a large estate, but of a country seat of about 2½ acres, provided with a garden, with vines, figs, and other good trees, and a pond.

man," who is respectful of established authority and just, since *maat* (which means truth, justice, rightness) is part of that world order of which his royal master is the champion. The "silent man"[20] is, therefore, not the meek sufferer, but the wise, self-possessed, well-adapted man, modest and self-effacing up to a point, but deliberate and firm in the awareness that he is thoroughly in harmony with the world in which he lives.

We cannot draw a corresponding picture of the common people of Egypt. Since they were illiterate, they are known to us only in descriptions of peasant life from the schools of scribes; and these are tendentious, singing the advantages of a "soft" job as an encouragement to the pupils involved in the arduous task of mastering the script. Notwithstanding the smug complacency of these texts and the evident satisfaction which the writers found in parodying every employment other than their own, the section dealing with the peasantry is worth quoting since it pictures well enough the farmer's lot under inefficient or corrupt administrators:

Remember you not the condition of the cultivator faced with the registering of the harvest tax, when the snake has carried off half the corn and the hippopotamus has devoured the rest? The mice abound in the fields. The locusts descend. The cattle devour. The sparrows bring disaster upon the cultivator. The remainder that is on the threshing floor is at an end, it falls to the thieves. The value of the hired cattle (?) is lost. The yoke of oxen has died while threshing and ploughing.

And now the scribe lands on the river bank and is about to register the harvest tax. The janitors carry staves and the Nubians (policemen) rods of palm, and they say, "Hand over the corn," though there is none. The cultivator is

[20] H. Frankfort, *Ancient Egyptian Religion* (New York, 1948), Chapter iii.

beaten all over, he is bound and thrown into the well, soused, and dipped head downwards. His wife has been bound in his presence, his children are in fetters. His neighbours abandon him and are fled.[21]

If such brutality had been the rule, it is clear that Egyptian society could not have survived. Agriculturalists are inevitably the prey of occasional calamities because they are dependent on weather and water. But if disasters follow one another frequently without relief, or if oppression by those in power exceeds a certain limit, there is no inducement for the peasant to continue his labours at all. He takes to flight or to revolt. We have seen why the texts used in the scribal schools emphasized the shadow-side of the peasant's lot. Moreover, we should remember that the humdrum normal life of the rural population offered no interest to the *literati*. The elementary satisfactions of a life wedded to nature, its crafty game of hiding assets from the bureaucrats, its tough endurance of injustice, the latent power of its indispensability—all these did not supply the scribal schools with material for the florid compositions which were their pride.

It was otherwise with the sculptors and painters. These men, charged with depicting on the walls of the great tombs the various rural activities from which the sustenance of the owner, in the next world, as in this, derived,[22] rendered these with the liveliest interest. Their work (Figs. 29, 30) presents to us a gay, light-hearted people, resembling in many respects the modern fellahin who similarly live on the verge of poverty under hardship and oppression. In the tombs we

[21] Gardiner in *Journal of Egyptian Archaeology*, XXVII (1941), 19.

[22] This is an over-simplified description of the significance of the scenes of daily life found in the tombs. For a more penetrating treatment, see H. A. Groenewegen-Frankfort, *Arrest and Movement*, 28–44.

see fishermen and herdsmen at their tasks, joking with one another (the words are sometimes rendered over their images). Harvesters move in a row, rhythmically swinging their sickles to the tune of a song which is accompanied by a man with a long reed pipe (Fig. 29).[23] Women bring food to their menfolk; two little girls squabble, while a third draws a thorn from the foot of her friend; a shepherd dozes under a tree, his dog asleep beside him (Fig. 30);[24] another herdsman refreshes himself from a goatskin bottle.

[23] Fig. 29, a relief from the Old Kingdom, shows, in the upper register, the harvesters with their sickles; on the extreme left is an overseer; the third figure from the left plays a long pipe, while his companion sings, holding the side of his face, as oriental singers do to this day. In the second register donkeys are brought to carry the harvest home. The register below shows various incidents in the transport; the bottom register shows how the sheaves are stacked.

[24] Fig. 30, a wall painting from the New Kingdom, is best "read" from the bottom upwards. At the left bottom corner teams of oxen draw ploughs, while sowers, holding a bag with seeds, sprinkle the grain with uplifted hands. Farther to the right men are shown breaking the ground with hoes. Behind the three of them shown on the right we see a girl drawing a thorn out of the foot of her friend.

The second register from below shows the grain being cut—one of the labourers takes a swig from a water jar handed him by a girl who stands in front, a basket hanging from her shoulder. Farther to the right the grain is carried away in hampers (underneath one of these, two girl gleaners are fighting and tearing each other's hair); and, on the far right, it is forked out in readiness for threshing. The threshing is done by bullocks who trample the grain—this is shown at the extreme right of the third register from below. To the left women winnow the grain, their hair wrapped in white cloth against the dust. The tomb owner watches in a kiosk and receives two water jars. Behind the kiosk squat the scribes who note the yield of the harvest while the grain is shovelled into heaps.

The upper register shows the deceased in his function as "Scribe of the fields of the Lord of the Two Lands." On the left are shown a group of his officials, dressed in white, pencase in hand, busy measuring the grain on the stalk; their attendants (with bare bodies) hold the measuring cord. A peasant (fol-

None of these people was free; not a single Egyptian was, in our sense of the word, free. No individual could call in question a hierarchy of authority which culminated in a living god. But it must not be forgotten that the reverse of freedom, isolation of the individual with or without "inalienable rights," was likewise lacking in Egypt. And servitude loses much of its sting if authority rests with those to whom faith has attributed the power of safeguarding the existence of society. Moreover, if it was true that all were at the disposal of the divine ruler and his officials, it was also true that even the lowliest might appeal to him[25] and claim what was "right"—*maat* (justice, right, and truth)—by which the ruler and the other gods were said to live and which informed, or was supposed to inform, his functionaries.

There were no castes, and men of simple origin might rise to the highest posts. The life-story of one Uni under three successive kings of the Sixth Dynasty shows that even lower officials, without influential relations, could rise to the highest offices once their ability and integrity had been recognized. The talented and industrious were not frustrated by a rigid class distinction or by a colour bar. A Nubian, frankly calling himself Panehsi, "the Nubian," or "negro," might be found in the highest places. The educated men were assigned by Pharaoh to whatever offices he

---

lowed by his wife who carries a basket on her head with further gifts) offers something to the tax officials, to propitiate them. But on the right, before the kiosk of the tomb owner and near the mooring-place of the boat which brought his subordinates to the scene, a peasant, who apparently defaulted, is beaten, while another kneels and prays for grace.

[25] "The Eloquent Peasant" is a tale of such an appeal. See *Journal of Egyptian Archaeology*, IX (1923), 7 ff., and a short discussion in my *Ancient Egyptian Religion*, 46, 146–50. For the conception of *maat*, ibid., 49–58.

thought fit. The common people were mostly tied to the land which they tilled for their own living and for the maintenance of the state. We do not know whether or not they were serfs. We do know that they had to turn in a considerable proportion of their produce as taxes and that they were liable to *corvée*. A proportion of the young men of all villages and estates was levied for the army, which was really a militia, but functioned much more frequently as a labour corps, available for all kinds of public works. It was this " army " which was sent on quarrying and mining expeditions, which dug the canals and built the temples and the royal tombs. If additional labour was needed to undertake special tasks or to expedite those in hand, the population at large could be drafted. For instance, the number of men required for the building of pyramids ran into many thousands, and it is likely that the stonecutters and their crews of unskilled helpers worked continuously in the quarries, the masons and their navvies on the site, but that during the inundation special levies were drafted to transport the stone from Tura, on the east bank, to Gizeh or Saqqara on the west bank of the Nile. For this purpose it was convenient that in summer, when the arable land was flooded, all agricultural labour came to a standstill, and the water covering the fields facilitated transport to the very foot of the desert plateau.[26]

We have some evidence of the life which these labourers lived. Three places are known where workmen were housed. Near the pyramid of Chephren at Gizeh there are, around a court, extensive barracks consisting of ninety-one galleries, each 88 feet long, 9½ feet wide, and 7 feet high. Petrie estimated that

---

[26] For a detailed discussion of the building of the pyramids, see I. E. S. Edwards, *The Pyramids of Egypt*, Pelican Books, chapter vii.

these could house 4000 men. Near the pyramid of Senusert II at Lahun there is a walled town covering an area 900 by 1200 feet. And at Tell el Amarna, near the northern group of rock tombs, is a walled village measuring only 210 by 210 feet (Fig. 31).[27] Its layout is dreary, with identical houses built back to back along straight streets. Each house consists of a court serving for kitchen and workshop, a central room as living-room, and two little bedrooms at the back. The enclosure wall has but one gate, opening on a square where the men no doubt mustered before being marched off to work. At one end of the square there is a larger house for the foreman or commandant. Described in this way the settlement makes the impression of a penal colony. But when one visits the site or reads the excavation report with some care, that impression changes. One is struck by the variations which one observes in going from house to house. Although the plans are identical, the tenants had made many changes to suit their individual needs and predilections. The internal arrangements are hardly ever the same. The objects found in the houses also show considerable variety and do not suggest penury or gloom. In one room was discovered a gay, painted frieze of dancing figures of the god Bes, the popular genius of music and love. One gets a distinct impression at the site that lack of freedom neither interfered with the home life of these workers nor destroyed their gaiety.

Abuses naturally existed. Royal decrees granting freedom from *corvée*, or levy, to the personnel of certain shrines explicitly protected these men against removal to other parts of the country, and show inci-

---

[27] T. Eric Peet and C. Leonard Woolley, *The City of Akhenaten,* Part I (38th Memoir of the Egypt Exploration Society), London, 1923.

dentally that common folk were exposed to this hazard. The small man was dependent on the protection of a man of influence whose client he might become if he was not already his serf. At this distance of time we cannot distinguish grades of servitude. It has been suggested that the best land of the large estates was worked with serfs while the less productive fields were let out to peasants who paid a fixed rent in produce; but the categories are not clearly distinguishable. Slaves, however, as distinct from serfs, did not play an important part in the economy of Egypt. It is doubtful whether they were kept in any numbers at all before the New Kingdom.[28] At that time the Syrian campaigns resulted in large numbers of captives who were used on royal and temple domains and in stone quarries. In earlier times captive Nubians may have been employed occasionally, but such isolated slaves served in families or at court as domestics, entertainers, dancers, or musicians and lived (one suspects) very much like the other servants. It has been pointed out[29] that the successful growing of grain requires a personal interest on the part of the cultivator, which slave labour lacks.

The craftsmen, too, were usually serving some great lord. Large numbers were employed by the king. We know, in fact, that the country was drained of talent for the benefit of the royal residence. The graves at Qau el Kebir—a cemetery in Middle Egypt used throughout the third millennium—show the scantiest equipment, and that of the poorest quality of craftsmanship, during the flourishing period of the Old Kingdom when the pyramids were being built. When

[28] Gardiner in *Zeitschrift für Aegyptische Sprache*, XLIII (1906), 43.

[29] Max Weber, *Gesammelte Aufsätze zur Sozial und Wirtschaftsgeschichte* (Tübingen, 1924), 24.

the central government had collapsed in the First Intermediate period, both the quality and the intrinsic value of the grave goods at Qau increased greatly. When craftsmen worked for the court, it is almost certain that they, too, were not free agents selling their wares or their services where they pleased. But we must, once more, guard against exaggerating their lot; they were not slaves. We happen, for instance, to know something of the extensive linen factories of Pharaoh. Under the Sixth Dynasty a royal weaving establishment in the north was under the management of one Seneb, a dwarf who, having worked himself up from the ranks, married a woman of the class of "Royal Kinsman" and could afford to build himself a fine tomb at Gizeh, from which we get our information.[30] One of the scenes in this tomb depicts the giving of rewards to Seneb's subordinates;[31] they receive headbands and necklaces, and this is significant, for these ornaments resemble in form the "gold" with which Pharaoh honoured officials of special merit. Let us assume that the jewellery with which the weavers were rewarded was less costly and consisted of bronze and fayence. It is nevertheless clear that the award was by no means a payment but a kind of gift which it was an honour to receive. Now it is noteworthy that the recipients depicted in Seneb's tomb are not all overseers and foremen, but also men and women who are merely mentioned by name, without title, and who therefore must be assumed to be simple weavers.

Craftsmen also worked for officials and on the large estates which came into being towards the end of the Old Kingdom. Such estates, like the royal domains, and the temple estates of later times, were self-sufficient economic units. Each had its own wharves, for

[30] Junker, *Giza*, V (Wien, 1941).
[31] *Op. cit.*, 52 ff.

instance,[32] where Nile boats were built and repaired. These served not only as ferries, but for every trip of any length which the owner had to undertake and for the shipment of grain, cattle, and other dues to the magazines of the Exchequer. They were used, furthermore, for shipments of supplies to the funerary establishments of past members of the family who might be buried near Memphis in a royal cemetery. When the weakening of the central power, to which we have referred, and the concurrent rise of a landed gentry, made it more and more customary for high officials to be buried in rock-cut tombs near their estates in the provinces, the equipment of these tombs was supplied by masons, cabinet-makers, jewellers, and so on, employed on the estate. There were, moreover, hunters, who not only killed game, but caught it to be fattened for the table; several kinds of antelopes, cranes, and even hyenas were treated in this way. Fishermen and fowlers were also employed, for wild geese and duck, fattened in the barnyard, were consumed in large numbers. Fish was dried and kept, but it was probably largely used as rations for labourers.

As regards the cultivators, whether they worked for a private estate, for a temple, or on a royal domain, they had to pay imposts of many kinds, and the hamlets and villages were collectively responsible in the person of their head man; this worthy had to produce the stipulated amounts on the day of reckoning or he risked a beating. The craftsmen, too, were organized in groups of five or ten men under a foreman who received their rations of food, clothing, and raw materials and was responsible for their work. Similar groups of men, working in shifts of one month, functioned as " hour priests " in the temples and funerary chapels. When they took over, their foremen received

[32] Junker, *Giza*, IV (Wien, 1940).

the inventory and were responsible for its proper maintenance.

The material basis of the Egyptian commonwealth was agriculture, regulated by the unaltering rhythm of the inundation. The names of the three seasons (of four months each) which the Egyptians distinguished were "Inundation" (middle of July to middle November), "Coming Forth" (of the seeds, or possibly of the land from the inundation, from Middle November to middle March), and "Drought." The conditions prevailing in prehistoric times, described in the second chapter, were not materially altered during the Old Kingdom. Land had to be reclaimed from the marshes. We have seen that the first king, Menes, undertook such work on a considerable scale. But the more the valley was drained, the more the need arose to distribute the inundation water so that it reached all the fields. From the beginning of the First Dynasty annual records of the height of the Nile were kept; their purpose can only have been to provide a basis for an estimate of its extent and thereby of the probable yield of the harvest. The digging of canals and the building of dikes was normally done by the central government, but there are some indications that the king encouraged the nomarchs to reclaim land by granting them the new fields which they then were allowed to settle with people from their estates. In the First Intermediate period when each nomarch had to take care of his area as best he could, one of them records:

I stocked villages in this nome that were enfeebled with cattle and men of other nomes, and those who had been serfs elsewhere I made rank as notables.[33]

The annual inundation with its fertilizing deposit of silt made manuring and rotation of crops unnecessary.

[33] After Griffith, *Deir el Gebrawi,* II, 30.

The tax records distinguish between low land, which was regularly inundated, and high land, which came under water only when the flood was high. This land was used for grazing or truck gardening. The bulk of the arable land was left soft by the retreating inundation and could be worked with primitive wooden hoes and ploughs. Animals, mostly sheep, were used to tread in the seed, and this had to be done speedily after the land had emerged but before it became hard and dry. Six-rowed barley and emmer wheat were the main crops. Lettuce, onions, beans, and lentils were, in antiquity as now, important secondary products. Ricinus plants were grown for oil, and flax for linen.

When the grain had grown to a certain height, surveyors measured it to assess it for taxation on an estimated yield (Fig. 30). It was harvested with sickles, threshed on a circular threshing floor by asses (and later by cattle) who trod out the kernels. As a rule, women did the winnowing by throwing the grain up in a winnowing basket. After that it was stored in barns or in beehive-shaped silos, and the portion due to the king or to the estate-owner was handed over. Large estates, including the royal domains and the temples, had reserves to supplement bad harvests. Seed-corn was lent to the tenants, and teams of oxen and asses for ploughing or carrying were lent or let out, too. There are records of great landowners relieving tenants who could not meet their obligations in difficult years.

But not only the grain harvest was taxed. There was a tax on canals and ponds, on trees and wells. The produce of the home industries and of the spare-time occupations of the people were taxed: they had to turn over some of their textiles, leatherwork, honey, oil, wine, vegetables, some of the catch of the fowler and fisherman, some of the increase of the shepherd's flock. Genesis xlvii. 24 states that one-fifth of all produce was owed to the government; this may or may not be correct; it is not improbable. Certain people were liable to pay fixed quantities of produce, irrespective of yield.

Again, it is necessary to correct our first reaction to a description of these conditions. In Egypt personal enterprise was made subsidiary to the performance of public duties; and it would seem that under normal conditions sufficient scope for private initiative, in production and in barter, remained. The contents of graves which are best, perhaps, called lower middle class (since of the poorest people no trace survives) show as much. It is likewise revealing that during Egypt's long history no attempts to overthrow the existing order were made. This shows that the Egyptian experiment of organizing a rural community was, on the whole, successful. The obligation to hand over part of every kind of produce may seem pettifogging to us. But money was unknown; the state could function only if it disposed of all kinds of articles to supply those who were in its service. If officials abused their power and oppressed the people, the peasants had an effective weapon at their disposal: they fled. This was a catastrophe for their owner since he remained liable for the normal dues on his land, which now lay deserted. The case is concisely put in a letter written by a steward to his master who was responsible for the management of a certain royal domain:

Another communication for my Lord's good pleasure, to the effect that two of the field labourers of the *mine* land of Pharaoh which is under my Lord's authority, have fled before the face of the stable-master Neferhotep, he having beaten them. And now, look, the fields of the *mine* land of Pharaoh which are under my Lord's authority are abandoned and there is no one to till them. This letter is for my Lord's information.[34]

A somewhat patriarchal relationship between master and men persists in many rural districts of old countries even to-day. A certain amount of arbitrariness, even of despotism, is taken for granted in the great; it is their privilege, but only if it is counterbalanced by a sense of responsibility for the land and for those who till it.

We may, therefore, accept as inherently probable such statements as the following, made by an Upper Egyptian nomarch who had taken matters in his own hands in the First Intermediate period.

I was one who computed (carefully) the consumption of Lower Egyptian grain. . . . I made a canal for this town when Upper Egypt was in a bad way, and one did not see any water. . . . I made high fields into marsh, I made the Nile inundate wasteland. . . . Whoever needed water got Nile water as he desired. . . . I was great in Lower Egyptian grain (barley) when the country was in tribulation. I was the one who fed the town with measure and bushel. I made the small man and his wife carry away Lower Egyptian grain and (likewise) the widow and her son. I had all imposts reduced which I found registered (as arrears) from the time of my father.[35]

Another nomarch, at Crocodilopolis in Upper Egypt, south of Thebes, reports:

I fed the "island in the river" (Crocodilopolis) during years of drought when 400 men were (in penury) there. I did not take away a man's daughter nor his field. I acquired ten flocks of goats with people to take care of them, two herds of cattle and one of asses. I bred small livestock. I obtained thirty boats of one kind and thirty of another

[34] Gardiner, *Journal of Egyptian Archaeology*, XXVII (1941), 22.

[35] After Kees, *Kulturgeschichte*, 40.

and brought Upper Egyptian grain to Hermonthis and Asphynis after Crocodilopolis was taken care of. The nome of Thebes came upstream (*i.e.* to obtain grain from me), but Crocodilopolis never sent downstream nor upstream (for grain) to another nome.[36]

The last inscription makes much of livestock, and stock-breeding was next in importance to agriculture. We have seen that a special official, "The Master of the King's Largesse," was in charge of its supervision. In antiquity, in contrast with now, plenty of marsh-land was available for grazing in the valley, and the large herds were also sent to the Delta in spring to graze. One official of the Sixth Dynasty lists 1000 head of cattle, 760 asses, 2200 goats, and nearly 1000 sheep as his own.

Trade played a subordinate part in the internal economy of the country. There was, naturally, a great deal of barter between individuals. There were markets where food, especially garden produce, or birds netted in the fields, or fish, were exchanged for tools or sandals or walking-sticks, necklaces, textiles or oils—luxuries or articles which, although issued by the estate office, might not, in quantity or quality, suit everyone. Barter in the market-place allowed a man to adjust his share in various goods to his own particular taste or to dispose of catches or produce obtained on the side. These markets are sometimes depicted in the tombs, and we know that already, in the Old Kingdom, pieces of metal served as standards of value. An important object was said to be worth so and so many rings. In the New Kingdom this system was simplified, and the value of an object was said to be so much weight (deben) of gold, silver, or copper. In the New Kingdom, too, the closer contact with Syria made more imported articles available for the market

[36] *Ibid.*, 41.

trade. A tomb-painting shows a Phoenician ship just made fast at the quay of Thebes. Some of the crew have gone ashore and approach booths where sandals, linen, fruits, and vegetables can be exchanged for a jug of Syrian oil or wine. This type of trade remained, however, purely marginal to the economy of Egypt. Neither the home-grown staple products nor the main imports were distributed through the markets. We do not meet the word "merchant" until the second millennium B.C., when it designates the official of a temple privileged to trade abroad.

Raw materials which Egypt lacked were procured through royal expeditions, organized by the Exchequer (which included among its personnel interpreters to assist the commanders in various foreign countries).[37] These expeditions were of two types. In Nubia, the eastern and western desert, and in Sinai, the nomad tribes and poor peasants could not oppose the Egyptians in any way at all. The army came and took what it needed. On quarrying and mining expeditions the military component of the expedition was no more than an armed escort, while the bulk of the "army" (as it was called) consisted of navvies to assist a core of trained stone-cutters or miners.

Another type of expedition was required to obtain wood from the Lebanon and frankincense and myrrh from Punt, the Somali coast. These lands were outside the sphere of Egyptian military influence, and the native rulers could ask for a price. This was offered in the form of royal presents to favourite vassals, and their products were listed as tribute. In reality there was an exchange; some splendid and extremely costly Egyptian jewellery, inscribed with the names of Pharaohs of the Twelfth Dynasty, has been found in tombs

[37] Gardiner, *Proceedings of the Society of Biblical Archaeology*, XXXVII (1915), 117; XXXIX (1917), 133.

of the local princes of Byblos at the foot of the Lebanon. Coniferous roofing beams in the tombs of the
First Egyptian Dynasty and a record of a sea expedition of Snefru of the Fourth Dynasty prove the great
age of this lumber trade with the Levant. And from a
late period we have the following list of objects which
an Egyptian envoy—Wenamon—offered in exchange
for wood from the Lebanon:

Five gold and five silver vessels; ten garments of royal
linen; ten pieces of other linen; five hundred pieces of fine
paper; five hundred cattle skins; five hundred ropes; twenty
bags of lentils; thirty baskets of fish.

The Phoenician export included, besides wood, oil,
wine, resin, and ivory.

It has been said that Pharaoh was the only whole-
sale merchant in Egypt and that foreign trade was a
royal monopoly. But the implication of profit-making
and exploitation is inappropriate. It was merely due to
the complete consistency with which the Egyptians
had organized their community as a centralized monarchy that they supplied themselves with the foreign
materials of which they stood in need by means of
royal expeditions. It is curious evidence of the practical effectiveness of Pharaonic rule that the absolute
monarchy of Egypt did supply essential commodities,
whether imported or produced at home, to the people
as a whole in sufficient quantities; the distribution took
place " from above," the king making gifts and allotments to his officials who in turn rewarded their re-
tainers and so down the social scale. And in the First
Intermediate period, when royal power suffered an
eclipse, the texts contain a complaint that there is no
wood available for the making of coffins.

Whatever aspect of Egyptian society we have scru-
tinized, we have found Pharaoh at the centre. Yet

nothing would be more misleading than to picture the Egyptians in abject submission to their absolute ruler. Their state can be described as " a self-directed organism held together by a common regard for customary rights and obligations."[38] Their polity was not imposed but evolved from immemorial predilections, and was adhered to, without protest, for almost three thousand years. Similar predilections have, in fact, maintained the institution of divine kingship among Africans related to the ancient Egyptians down to our own days. It was good, not evil; it gave a sense of security which the Asiatic contemporaries of the ancient Egyptians totally lacked. If a god had consented to guide the nation, society held a pledge that the unaccountable forces of nature would be well disposed and bring prosperity and peace. Nor does the Egyptian view lack ethical content. Truth, justice, were "that by which the gods live," an essential element in the established order. Hence Pharaoh's rule was not tyranny, nor his service slavery.

[38] F. M. Powicke, *The Reformation in England* (Oxford, 1941), 31.

APPENDIX

The Influence of Mesopotamia on Egypt
Towards the End of the Fourth Millennium B.C.[1]

THE PROBLEM to which we turn now has been discussed intermittently for the last fifty years, but in the earlier discussions preconceived ideas played a considerable part. For while it is admitted that intercourse stimulates individuals, it is often believed that granting foreign influence to have affected a people is derogatory. The essential difference between mechanical copying and creative borrowing, between a slavish dependence on foreign examples and a free selection of congenial material, is entirely overlooked. Another circumstance, too, has militated against an unbiased weighing of the evidence. When our knowledge of the ancient Near East was fragmentary, it was habitual to explain changes in terms of conquest and immigration from some hypothetical, as yet unknown, region; but the extensive explorations which took place between the two world wars have discredited this type of explanation, and the supposed homelands of the newcomers proved, in cultural matters, to have been peripheral dependencies of the two great centres in Egypt and Mesopotamia. These, on the other hand, were seen to

[1] This subject has been studied in the works named on p. 124, n. 5. Since the last of these was published during the war and is hardly known abroad, we have included in this Appendix more matter dealt with on a previous occasion than would otherwise have been justifiable.

have been unusually resistant to foreign influence and capable of imposing conformity upon all comers.[2]

Our increased knowledge has thus induced an unwillingness to appeal to foreign influence or migrations as explanations of cultural changes. Now, however, the opposite viewpoint receives exaggerated emphasis, and we find students proudly proclaiming their ignorance of anthropology and emphasizing, without a critical examination of all the facts, the autonomy and self-containedness of the great cultural centres of the Near East.

Evidence obtained in the decade before the Second World War allows us, however, to solve the problem, at least as far as it concerns the formative phase of Egyptian civilization. For the discovery in Mesopotamia of remains of the Protoliterate period revealed the source from which curious and passing features of Egyptian culture in late predynastic and protodynastic times were obviously derived.

The strongest evidence of this contact between Mesopotamia and Egypt is supplied by three cylinder seals shown by their very material and by their designs to have been made in Mesopotamia during the second half of the Protoliterate period (Figs. 33, 34), but found in Egypt. One was excavated at Naqada (Fig. 32), in a Gerzean grave; and the same origin is probable for the other two.[3] These importations were not without consequence: from the beginning of the First Dynasty the cylinder seal was adopted in Egypt and made at once in considerable quantities. Since it is an odd form for a seal, used only in countries in contact with Mesopotamia, and since one of the Meso-

[2] Phrased differently, one might say that we had, without justification, used the expansion of the Indo-European and Arabic-speaking peoples as an analogy for the changes observed in Egypt and Mesopotamia.

[3] Frankfort, *Cylinder Seals* (London, 1939), 293.

potamian cylinders was found in Egypt in a context just ante-dating the earliest native seals, it would be perverse to deny that the Egyptians followed the Mesopotamian example. But it is quite characteristic for them that they exploited the new suggestion with the greatest freedom. They even used engraved cylinders for a purpose for which there is no Mesopotamian prototype: some of these objects, found in the graves of the First Dynasty, are not seals at all but funerary amulets showing the dead man at the table (Figs. 37, 38, 39).[4] In addition, the Egyptians used cylinders as seals, but they very rarely covered them with pictorial designs. They engraved upon them the names and titles of officials written in hieroglyphs (Figs. 35, 36). In Mesopotamia the earliest cylinders (Figs. 14–16, 42, 44) bear designs, not inscriptions; inscribed seals are unknown before the second Early Dynastic period, and then even the inscribed examples always bear a design as their distinctive feature. Moreover, the early Egyptian seals are usually made of wood, a material not used in Mesopotamia, as far as we know. Since, on the other hand, the cylinder was better adapted to the sealing of merchandise and clay tablets than to that of documents on papyrus, it was replaced in Egypt during the Middle Kingdom by the stamp seal in the shape of a scarab. The Egyptians, therefore, in no way copied slavishly the Mesopotamian invention, but adapted it to their own needs

[4] The reader unacquainted with these cylinders may identify the figures as follows. In Fig. 37 he will see some hieroglyphs which appear, reversed, at the extreme left in the impression of Fig. 38. To the right of them one sees the offering table with two crescents representing loaves of bread; over these a man extends his hand. He is seated on a bed with legs ending in bull's or lion's feet (such beds have been found in the graves at Abydos). His long hair is rendered in a crosshatched mass. In Fig. 39 is a similar figure, facing to the right. His hair is rendered with a straight line.

until such a time as they had discovered a more suitable form of seal.

In the field of art a somewhat similar development can be observed.[5] We can distinguish two groups of phenomena: motifs are taken over from Mesopotamian monuments of the Protoliterate period, or Egyptian motifs are composed in a manner which is, to judge by later usage, un-Egyptian and can be understood as a passing influence of Mesopotamian style. The most striking example of the copying of an alien, Mesopotamian, motif, is the group of the man dominating two lions on the Gebel el Arak knife-handle (Fig. 23). Such groups are common at all times in Mesopotamia but exceedingly rare in Egypt. And in the present case the derivation cannot be doubted: the hero between the lions copies in every detail of his appearance—his garment, his beard, his hair, wound round his head and bound up in a chignon at the back—the often recurring figure of the " leader " or king depicted on a granite stela from Erech and on numerous seals (Figs. 15, 44). Even the style of the figure, the way in which the muscles in the legs are rendered, for instance, is entirely un-Egyptian, as a comparison with the figures

[5] In order not to overload this Appendix with footnotes, we shall refer only to the most important monuments. These are conveniently collected in J. Capart, *Primitive Art in Egypt*, London, 1905. Detailed discussions with references will be found there and in the following three works: H. Frankfort, *Studies in Early Pottery of the Near East*, I (London, 1924), 117–42; A. Scharff, " Neues zur Frage der ältesten Aegyptish-Babylonischen Kulturbeziehungen " in *Zeitschrift für Aegyptische Sprache*, LXXI (1935), 89–106; H. Frankfort, " The Origin of Monumental Architecture in Egypt " in *American Journal of Semitic Languages and Literatures*, LVIII (1941), 329–58. In this last article, I have formulated disagreement with certain ideas propounded by Scharff, especially as regards cylinder seals, and have shown (*op. cit.*, 354, n. 55) that the relief of shell in Berlin (also depicted by Capart, *op. cit.*, 83, Figs. 50–1) is a purely Mesopotamian object, and therefore irrelevant to the present discussion.

on the other face of the knife-handle (Fig. 24) shows.

Other motifs on palettes and knife-handles likewise have Mesopotamian prototypes. The serpent-necked lions or panthers on the Narmer palette (Fig. 28) recur, identically intertwined, on seals of the early and late Protoliterate period (Fig. 16). Winged griffins (Fig. 40)[6] and intertwined snakes (Fig. 41)[7] are also at home in Mesopotamia from the Protoliterate period onwards and put in a passing appearance in Egypt.

Antithetical groups[8] and the carnivore attacking an impassive prey (Figs. 23, 40), are examples of Egyptian designs composed in an un-Egyptian manner.[9] We may even formulate the way in which they are un-Egyptian: they share with the group of the hero dominating two lions, the intertwined snakes and lions,

[6] They occur on the Small Hierakonpolis palette: Capart, *op. cit.*, Fig. 172.

[7] See also the University College knife-handle (Capart, *op. cit.*, 72, Fig. 37) and the Berlin knife-handle (Capart, *op. cit.*, 73, Fig. 38.)

[8] Gebel el Arak knife-handle (Fig. 23); Small Louvre palette (Capart, *op. cit.*, 235, Fig. 174); Lion palette (Capart, *op. cit.*, 239, Fig. 178 plus 241, Fig. 180); Zaki Youssef Saad, *Royal Excavations at Saqqara and Helwan, 1944–5, Supplément aux Annales du Service des Antiquités de l'Egypte,* 166, Fig. 14.

[9] The Egyptian manner of representing carnivores and their prey is shown in the central row of animals on the Hunters' palette (Fig. 25) where they appear in headlong flight. See also the Small Hierakonpolis palette and Egyptian renderings of the historical periods. In Mesopotamia the prey is rendered as unaffected by the attack; our Fig. 14, for instance, can be matched by a seal (Frankfort, *Cylinder Seals,* Plate V *a*) where a lion is shown striking his claws into a bull's hindquarters. The bull stands as in our figure. This is but one example from many. Another instance of this rendering in Egypt is found on a macehead from Hierakonpolis (Capart, *op. cit.*, 97, Fig. 68) with alternating dogs and lions, each of which attacks the one before him with teeth and claws. This type of design, a circular interlocking by activation of the individual figures, is characteristic for Mesopotamia and occurs on numerous cylinder seals, on the silver vase of Entemena, and on the macehead of Mesilim of Kish in the Louvre.

and the serpent-necked panthers a pronouncedly un-
realistic character. Animal forms are, in all these instances, used to produce a decorative design; they are
subjected to a purely aesthetic purpose. And though
the Egyptians eventually used plant motifs in such a
fashion, they never again so employed animal or
human figures. In Mesopotamia, on the other hand,
imagination and design usually prevailed over probability or nature.[10] Hence we see, once again, that the
Egyptians experimented with Mesopotamian inventions during the formative phase of their civilization
but soon rejected what was uncongenial.

There remain two fields in which Mesopotamian examples have produced results more important than
those we have discussed so far. They are architecture
and writing. With the First Dynasty, monumental
brick architecture makes its appearance in a form,
both as regards material and plan, which recalls the
Protoliterate temples of Mesopotamia.[11] It is a moot
point whether bricks were made in Egypt in prehistoric times. In Persia, Mesopotamia, and Asia Minor
(Mersin) they were used on a great scale from the Al
Ubaid period onwards, and were known even earlier.
In Egypt a few bricks have been found in prehistoric
context, but not actually in walls, and whether they
were used for buildings may well be doubted, since in
Nubia, where prehistoric culture continued to flourish
even after the accession of Menes, bricks were used
only at a later date. Moreover, a design on the Hunt-

[10] See Frankfort, *Cylinder Seals*, Epilogue *et passim*.

[11] See Frankfort, " The Origin of Monumental Architecture in
Egypt," in *American Journal of Semitic Languages and Literatures*, LVIII (1941), 329–58. In this article we have not only
discussed the detailed technical similarities between recessed
brick building in the two countries but also demonstrated the
inadequacy of prevalent explanations of the Egyptian examples,
" irrespective of the fact that they failed to account for the contemporary construction of similar buildings in Mesopotamia."

ers' Palette (Fig. 25), and hieroglyphs representing traditional palaces and shrines, indicate that predynastic public buildings were made of wood and matting, or perhaps of wattle and daub. It is likely that the palaces and other important buildings of the First Dynasty were still made of those materials.[12] But in this dynasty highly sophisticated brick architecture is suddenly used in the construction of graves.

In Egypt secular buildings were at all times less permanent than tombs and temples. When, from the Third Dynasty onwards, these were built of stone, houses and palaces were still built of brick. And this distinction holds good for all subsequent periods. Under the First Dynasty, when brick architecture came into its own, this new and more permanent architecture was used, at first, for the royal tombs which were decorated with buttresses and recesses on all four sides (Figs. 46, 47, 50). This ornamentation was achieved, in some cases (Fig. 46),[13] by the use of two kinds of bricks—large ones for the core of the building and smaller ones for the recessing. These small bricks are of a size and shape peculiar, in Mesopotamia, to the latter half of the Protoliterate period and were used in an identical fashion, three rows of stretchers alternating as a rule with one row of headers.[14] The recesses and buttresses duplicate exactly the recessing of Protoliterate temples. Other technical details—the manner in which a plinth or platform is constructed

[12] This does not imply that they must have been mean structures. In Uganda, for instance, no fewer than a thousand men are continuously engaged in the royal enclosure on building and repairs (John Roscoe, *The Baganda*, 366).

[13] See also Borchardt, "Das Grab des Menes," in *Zeitschrift für Aegyptische Sprache*, XXXVI (1898), 87–105.

[14] This is the *Riemchenverband*, observed by the excavators of Erech (E. Heinrich, *Schilf und Lehm*, 40) and of Tell Asmar (Delougaz and Lloyd, *Pre-Sargonid Temples in the Diyala Region* [Chicago, 1942], 169, Fig. 127).

(Fig. 47),[15] the use of short timbers inserted horizontally as the strengthening in the niches (Figs. 49, 50)—likewise reflect Mesopotamian usages of the Protoliterate period (Fig. 48).[16] In Mesopotamia the whole method of recessed brick building can be seen to come into being, starting with the temples at Eridu and Tepe Gawra of the Al Ubaid period (when the buttresses, widely spaced, seem merely to strengthen the walls), until, in the Protoliterate age (Fig. 45), the exact degree of complexity was reached with which brick building appears under the First Egyptian Dynasty, unheralded, and yet with every refinement of which the material is capable. Contemporary but simplified renderings of these buildings on Protoliterate cylinder seals in Mesopotamia resemble those on First Dynasty monuments in Egypt (Figs. 42, 43, 44).[17] There are differences, too, which indicate that the Mesopotamian renderings were not copied in Egypt, but that the Egyptian and Mesopotamian renderings are abbreviations of buildings which themselves were

[15] In our figure and in the tomb of Neithotep ("Das Grab des Menes"—see n. 2, above), the structures, like the Babylonian temples, appear to stand on a brick platform; but in reality a low revetment was built up against the outside of the walls after these had been built up—complete with recesses—from the foundations. In Babylonia this apparent platform is called a *kisu*.

[16] Our Fig. 48 shows the impressions of these round timbers in the brick work of the White Temple at Erech, of which Fig. 45 shows the plan. Fig. 49 shows a wooden sarcophagus found in a First Dynasty tomb at Tarkhan in Egypt, which imitates a recessed building with a similar strengthening of round timbers. Fig. 50 shows an actual tomb found at Abu Roash in Lower Egypt with some timbers still in place.

[17] The Egyptian designs (Figs. 42, 44 left, 43) are supposed to render a palace façade, an assumption incapable of proof and ignoring the fact that the tombs have recesses on all four sides. But whatever the original of this design may have been, its abbreviated rendering in Egypt resembles an abbreviated rendering of temples in Mesopotamia (Fig. 44 right) very closely.

closely alike. The towers appearing on the Stele of
Djet (Fig. 43) are found in the later part of the
Protoliterate period (Fig. 42 right). Entrance towers
with straight sides were, since Early Dynastic times, in
use in Mesopotamia but not in Egypt, where the pylon
with a pronounced batter was developed.

In view of this great variety of detailed resemblances there can be no reasonable doubt that the
earliest monumental brick architecture of Egypt was
inspired by that of Mesopotamia where it had a long
previous history. In conclusion, it is worth notice that
the architectural forms used in Mesopotamia for
temples were applied in Egypt to royal tombs and
royal castles.[18] But then, Pharaoh—in life and in death
—was a god. Stone architecture, so characteristic for
Egypt in historical times, replaced bricks in the royal
tombs from the Third Dynasty onward.

We must turn, finally, to the invention of hiero-
glyphic writing. It is a moot point whether it first appears on the macehead of Scorpion (Fig. 26), or
whether the two signs on the Hunters' palette (Fig.
25) must count as writing. These cannot be read, although they may mean " shrine of (the earth-god)
Akeru," for this name is written with the double fore-
quartered animal in the pyramid texts. Whether this
palette or the Scorpion mace is the first inscribed
monument, the appearance of writing falls within a
period in which Mesopotamian influence has been
proved to exist.

It has been customary to postulate prehistoric antecedents for the Egyptian script, but this hypothesis has
nothing in its favour.[19] In the annals of the kingdom

[18] At Abydos three of these, perhaps built under the Second
Dynasty, survive. See Petrie, *Abydos*, III (London, 1904),
Plates V–VIII.

[19] Scharff, *Archaeologische Beiträge zur Frage der Entstehung
der Hieroglyphenschrift* (München, 1942).

(which happen to survive in a version of the Fifth Dynasty), events are recorded only from the First Dynasty onwards, a fact suggesting that no written records of earlier times existed. Only some names of prehistoric chieftains were still known and entered in the annals as " kings " preceding Menes.[20]

But the writing which appeared without antecedents at the beginning of the First Dynasty was by no means primitive. It has, in fact, a complex structure. It includes three different classes of signs: ideograms, phonetic signs, and determinatives.[21] This is precisely the

[20] See *Kingship and the Gods*, 20 and 350, n. 15.

[21] We have shown that in early Mesopotamian script words sounding alike (*e.g.* " to live " and " arrow ") could be written with the same sign and the meaning clarified by the addition of determinatives which were not pronounced but indicated what kind of notion was rendered. In Egypt from the first we find the same devices in use. The hieroglyph depicting a rib can also be used to render the verb " to approach," in which case two legs are added as a determinative. Just as in Mesopotamia the picture of the arrow became a phonetic sign for *ti*, so the Egyptian signs become phonetic signs. There is, however, a difference. In Mesopotamia both consonants and vowels were rendered by the signs. In Egypt the vowels were ignored, and only the consonantal skeleton of the word was rendered. This was natural to the Egyptians, because the consonants of their words remained constant while the vowels changed in the conjugation and declension (as with us the verb " to break " has in the past tense " he broke "). To turn to our example, the picture of the rib stood for *spir* when it meant rib, *soper* when it meant " to approach," and so on. (This is the vocalization in Coptic, the latest stage of Egyptian which used the Greek alphabet and, therefore, wrote vowels.) The phonetic value of the sign of the rib is therefore *spr*. In this way the Egyptians adapted the notion of how language might be rendered (which they evidently got from Mesopotamia) to the peculiarities of their own language. I do not want to suggest that Egyptian necessarily calls for a script in which only the consonants are written. Scharff (*loc. cit.*), points out that Hebrew and Arabic developed in their punctuation a method of rendering the changing vocalization alongside the permanent consonantal skeleton of the words.

Some of the phonetic signs of Egyptian consist of only one consonant. In a discussion concerned with Egyptian writing

same state of complexity which had been reached in Mesopotamia at an advanced stage of the Protoliterate period. There, however, a more primitive stage is known in the earliest tablets, which used only ideograms. To deny, therefore, that Egyptian and Mesopotamian systems of writing are related amounts to maintaining that Egypt invented independently a complex and not very consistent system at the very moment of being influenced in its art and architecture by Mesopotamia where a precisely similar system had just been developed from a more primitive stage. To state this view is, of course, to reject it.

But, again, the Egyptians did not copy the Mesopotamian system slavishly; they were merely stimulated to develop a script of their own, once the notion that language could be rendered graphically had been conveyed. The writing signs—the "hieroglyphs"—which they invented have nothing at all in common with the Mesopotamian signs. They depict Egyptian objects; they depict them faithfully; and they remain to the end exact pictures in the majority of cases. In Mesopotamia the tendency to use abstract symbols was strong from the beginning, and prevailed at an early date. And before the middle of the third millennium even the pictograms had lost all trace of semblance to the objects they originally rendered (Fig. 13). This contrast between the Egyptian and Mesopotamian scripts undoubtedly has a twofold cause. The Egyptians always loved the pictorial rather than the abstract and had a strong inclination towards the concrete. This tendency (which also prevented them from dis-

---

there would be no reason why they should be mentioned in particular, since they do not differ in principle from the other signs. But in a wider historical context the signs with the value of a single consonant are of unique importance: they seem to be the distant ancestors of the alphabet.

torting animal forms for the sake of ornamental schemes) made them adopt and retain minute images as writing signs. But, in the second place, writing was at first used in Egypt for a purpose different from that to which the Mesopotamians put it. In Mesopotamia writing was invented to serve the practical needs of administration. In Egypt it was used, at first, as an element of monumental art, in the form of legends added to reliefs (Figs. 26, 27, 28).

The legends fixed the identity of the figures in the reliefs which could be made explicit only by the adding of names and titles. But once writing was introduced, it was—in Egypt also—used for practical purposes; and this required a shorter and more cursive script. In the tomb of Djet, the fourth king of the First Dynasty, a note in cursive script has been discovered;[22] and it has been pointed out[23] that documents must have been in common use in the Second Dynasty since the sign of the papyrus roll, tied up and sealed, is used from then on. For monumental inscriptions, however, the pictorial hieroglyphs were used even under the Roman emperors.

In view of the doubt which persists in many quarters, it seems worth while to represent the evidence for Mesopotamian influence in Egypt at about 3000 B.C.—excluding writing—in a table which shows that we are confronted, not by a few random resemblances, but by a group of related phenomena. And this is, in fact, corroborated by the observation that the foreign features in Egypt all derive from one and the same phase of Mesopotamian civilization, namely, the later part of the Protoliterate period.[24] Now this phase (formerly

[22] Petrie, *Royal Tombs*, I, Plate 19, No. 11.

[23] Scharff, *op. cit.*, 55.

[24] Some features of Mesopotamian civilization remain almost unaltered during the Protoliterate period, hence it is very im-

called after Jamdat Nasr) represents an age of expansion: a richly equipped temple was built at Brak in Northern Syria (see above, p. 84); Mesopotamian tablets were found not only at Susa in Elam but at Sialk near Kashan in Central Persia (Fig. 51); and Mesopotamian cylinders were found, not only at the places mentioned just now, but as far afield as Cappadocia and Troy. At a time when Mesopotamian influence radiated in all directions it was but natural that it should touch Egypt also. Thus the traces of

---

portant that the Egyptian links can be proved to derive from the latter part, which is known to be a time of expansion in any case. The evidence for the synchronization of the rise of Dynasty I in Egypt with the later part of the Protoliterate period in Mesopotamia consists of three groups:

(a) The cylinder seals found in Egypt all belong to the "Jamdat Nasr" style and do not include any of the earlier style, known from seal impressions found in Archaic Layer IV at Erech. Likewise absent are examples of the brocade style which succeeds the Jamdat Nasr style in Early Dynastic I. Thus the upper and lower limits of the period during which contact took place are defined.

(b) The small bricks used in recessing at Naqada and Saqqara (Fig. 46) are predominant in the later part of the Protoliterate period in Mesopotamia. In the earlier part larger bricks are commonly used; in the subsequent Early Dynastic period the bricks are plano-convex.

(c) During the Protoliterate period Mesopotamian buildings were decorated all around with elaborate recesses (Figs. 45, 48); and this is the decoration found in the earliest monumental buildings in Egypt, the tombs at Naqada, Abydos, Saqqara, etc. In Early Dynastic Mesopotamia simplified recessing all around became the style; and the multiple recessing was reserved for towers flanking temple entrances (Fig. 19). These towers are introduced in Mesopotamia in the later half of the Protoliterate period as a seal impression shows (Fig. 42 right). The abbreviated renderings of recessed buildings in Egypt show both flat buildings and buildings with towers (Fig. 42, left; 43, 44), a combination which corresponds neither with the earlier part of the Protoliterate period nor with the Early Dynastic period in Mesopotamia but only with the later part of the Protoliterate period. Again, the upper and lower limits of the period of contact are defined.

Mesopotamian arts and crafts which we find in pre- and protodynastic Egypt represent but one more manifestation of the expansion of Mesopotamia during the latter part of the Protoliterate period.

MESOPOTAMIAN INFLUENCE IN PRE- AND PROTODYNASTIC EGYPT

I. EVIDENCE OUTSIDE THE FIELD OF ART.

A. *Mesopotamian Objects found in Egypt.*

1. Three cylinder seals of the late Protoliterate period.

B. *Mesopotamian Usages temporarily adopted in Egypt.*

1. Sealing with engraved cylinders.
2. Recessed brick building for monumental purposes.

C. *Mesopotamian Objects depicted on Egyptian Monuments.*

1. Costume, on the Gebel el Arak knife-handle.
2. Scalloped battle-axe on fragment of late predynastic stone vase.[25]
3. Ships, on Gebel el Arak knife-handle, " decorated" vases, and ivory labels of First Dynasty.[26]

II. EVIDENCE IN THE FIELD OF ART.

A. *Mesopotamian Motifs depicted in Egypt.*

1. Composite animals, especially winged griffins and serpent-necked felines, on palettes and knife-handles.

[25] This object is depicted in Capart, *op. cit.*, 100, Fig. 70, and Scharff, *Die Altertümer der Vor- und Frühzeit Aegyptens*, II, Plate 22, No. 108.

[26] There are no parallels in Egypt in historical times for the ships with vertical prow and stern, while the Mesopotamian *belem*—represented in silver, *e.g.* in the Royal Tombs at Ur— assumes that shape. See Woolley, *The Royal Cemetery*, Plate 169, and, for older literature, Frankfort, *Studies in Early Pottery of the Near East*, I, 138 ff.

2. Group of hero dominating two lions, on Gebel el Arak knife-handle and in tomb at Hierakonpolis
3. Pairs of entwined animals, on knife-handles and Narmer palette.

B. *Mesopotamian peculiarities of Style apparent in Egypt.*

1. Antithetical group, on knife-handles and palettes.
2. Group of carnivore attacking impassive prey, on knife-handles.
3. Drawing of musculature, on Gebel el Arak knife-handle.

It would, however, be an error to see the birth of Egyptian civilization as a consequence of contact with Mesopotamia. The signs of change accumulating towards the end of the predynastic age are too numerous and the outcome of the change is too emphatically Egyptian in its general character and its particulars to allow us to speak of derivation or dependence. In fact, Mesopotamian influence can be entirely discounted—except in the field of writing—without altering in any essential respect the outcome of the change. We have said elsewhere that there is no necessity to assume Mesopotamian influence in order to explain the development of Pharaonic civilization, but it so happens that we have evidence that such influence was, in fact, exercised. We observe that Egypt, in a period of intensified creativity, became acquainted with the achievements of Mesopotamia; that it was stimulated; and that it adapted to its own rapid development such elements as seemed compatible with its efforts. It mostly transformed what it borrowed and after a time rejected even these modified derivations.

It is unfortunate that we cannot yet answer the question where and how contact between Egypt and Mesopotamia was established. We only know the time at which it took place. The signs of Sumerian influence point, one and all, to the Protoliterate period in Mesopotamia, and more especially to the latter half of that period; and they appear in Egypt towards the end of the Gerzean period and during the very beginning of the First Dynasty. This is, of course, an invaluable synchronism, even though it is still impossible to express it in exact dates. It may also have a bearing on the question in which locality contact was established.

In Egypt, signs of contact with Sumer almost cease after Narmer's reign; and since contact with Syria increased rather than diminished during the First Dynasty, it seems unlikely that the Mesopotamian influences reached Egypt from the north. The argument is not conclusive; we have seen that Sumerian culture moved upstream along the Tigris and Euphrates, and that a great temple was built at Brak on the Khabur in North Syria in Protoliterate times. But in Syria we do not find signs that native culture was deeply affected by contact with Sumer. This may be due to the incompleteness of our evidence; or it may be that Syrian culture was so unprogressive that it could not profit from such contact in the way Egypt demonstrably did. But before we accept this view we must consider an alternative.

It is possible that the Egyptians came into contact with Mesopotamia in the south, on the route which led from the Red Sea, past Southern Arabia, to the Persian Gulf. There are two arguments against this assumption: it has no analogy in historical times; and there is absolutely no sign of contact with Egypt to be found in Mesopotamia. But it is possible that the meeting-place was a region along the southern route, outside Sumer. In both Sumerian and Egyptian temples censing with aromatics was usual. In the time of

Herodotus, frankincense was used for this purpose in Babylon, but we do not know at what date this was first introduced. In Egypt frankincense was known very early; if that holds good for Sumer also, contact might have been established in the regions from which frankincense was obtained—Southern Arabia or the Somali coast. There missions might have met, or middlemen might have acquainted Egyptians with Sumerian achievements. We know that the route to the Red Sea from Egypt—through the Wadi Hammamat—was used at a very early date. Archaic statues of the god Min were found at Koptos at the Egyptian end of that route.[27] They belong to the end of the Gerzean period or to the First Dynasty, and bear designs scratched on their sides which include the sword of the swordfish and pteroceras shells, found in the Red Sea. But the bearing of these facts upon the question where contact between Egypt and Sumer took place must remain, for the moment, a matter of surmise.

[27] Petrie, *Koptos* (London, 1896), Plates III, IV, V 4; Capart, *loc. cit.*, 223, Fig. 166.

CHRONOLOGICAL TABLE

UPPER EGYPT	LOWER EGYPT	NORTH MESOPOTAMIA	SOUTH MESOPOTAMIA
Tasian Period		5000 ?	
	Fayum A	Hassunah Period	
Badarian Period		*Samarran*	
	Merimde	Halaf Period	
			Eridu
Amratian Period		Northern Ubaid Period	Southern Ubaid Period
			3900 ?
			Warka Period
			3750 ?
		Gawra Period	
Early Gerzean Period			Early Protoliterate Period
	Maadi		
Late Gerzean Period			Late Protoliterate Period
	3100		3100
Protodynastic Period: Dynasties	I	Ninevite Period	Early Dynastic Period
	II 2664		
Old Kingdom: Dynasties	III		
	IV		
	V		2425
			Proto-Imperial Period 2340
	VI 2181	North Akkadian Period	Dynasty of Akkad 2180

ANCHOR BOOKS

ANCIENT CIVILIZATION

ALBRIGHT, WILLIAM FOXWELL From the Stone Age to Christianity, A100

ARISTOPHANES Five Comedies of Aristophanes, trans. Rogers, A57

BURCKHARDT, JACOB The Age of Constantine the Great, A65

CASSON, LIONEL, ed. & trans. Selected Satires of Lucian, A295

COULANGES, FUSTEL DE The Ancient City, A76

CROSS, FRANK MOORE, JR. The Ancient Library of Qumran, A272

FORSTER, E. M. Alexandria: A History and a Guide, A231

FRANKFORT, HENRI The Birth of Civilization in the Near East, A89

FRAZER, J. G. The New Golden Bough, ed. Gaster, A270

GASTER, THEODOR H. The Dead Sea Scriptures, A92

—— Thespis: Ritual, Myth and Drama in the Ancient Near East, A230

GRAVES, ROBERT, ed. The Comedies of Terence, A305

HADAS, MOSES, trans. & ed. A History of Rome, A78

HOMER The Odyssey, trans. Fitzgerald, A333

KITTO, H. D. F. Greek Tragedy, A38

KRAMER, SAMUEL NOAH History Begins at Sumer, A175

——, ed. Mythologies of the Ancient World, A229

MOSCATI, SABATINO The Face of the Ancient Orient, A289

MURRAY, GILBERT Five Stages of Greek Religion, A51

NEHRU, JAWAHARLAL The Discovery of India, A200

PLAUTUS Six Plays of Plautus, trans. Casson, A367

SENECA The Stoic Philosophy of Seneca, trans. & ed. Hadas, A148

SOMERVILLE, JOHN, & SANTONI, RONALD, eds. Social and Political Philosophy: Readings from Plato to Gandhi, A370

TAYLOR, A. E. Socrates, A9

TREVELYAN, G. M. A History of England: Vol. I—From the Earliest Times to the Reformation, A22a

VIRGIL The Aeneid of Virgil, trans. Lewis, A20

WALEY, ARTHUR Three Ways of Thought in Ancient China, A75

WRIGHT, G. ERNEST, & FREEDMAN, DAVID NOEL, eds. The Biblical Archaeologist Reader, A250

ANCHOR BOOKS

MYTHOLOGY AND LEGEND

BEDIER, JOSEPH   The Romance of Tristan and Iseult, A2
COULANGES, FUSTEL DE   The Ancient City, A76
FRAZER, J. G.   The New Golden Bough, ed. Gaster, A270
KRAMER, SAMUEL NOAH, ed.   Mythologies of the Ancient World, A229
MALINOWSKI, BRONISLAW   Magic, Science and Religion, A23
MURRAY, GILBERT   Five Stages of Greek Religion, A51
MURRAY, MARGARET   The God of the Witches, A212
VIRGIL   The Aeneid of Virgil, trans. Lewis, A20
WESTON, JESSIE L.   From Ritual to Romance, A125

ANTHROPOLOGY AND ARCHAEOLOGY

ALBRIGHT, WILLIAM FOXWELL   From the Stone Age to Christianity, A100
BENDIX, REINHARD   Max Weber: An Intellectual Portrait, A281
COULANGES, FUSTEL DE   The Ancient City, A76
CROSS, FRANK MOORE, JR.   The Ancient Library of Qumran, A272
FRANKFORT, HENRI   The Birth of Civilization in the Near East, A89
FRAZER, J. G.   The New Golden Bough, ed. Gaster, A270
GASTER, THEODOR H.   The Dead Sea Scriptures, A92
HOWELLS, WILLIAM   Back of History, N34
KRAMER, SAMUEL NOAH   History Begins at Sumer, A175
——, ed.   Mythologies of the Ancient World, A229
MALINOWSKI, BRONISLAW   Magic, Science and Religion, A23
MURRAY, MARGARET   The God of the Witches, A212
TURNBULL, COLIN   The Lonely African, A374
WESTHEIM, PAUL   The Sculpture of Ancient Mexico/La Escultura Del Mexico Antiguo (Bilingual edition, trans. Bernard), A335
WESTON, JESSIE L.   From Ritual to Romance, A125
WRIGHT, G. ERNEST, & FREEDMAN, DAVID NOEL   The Biblical Archaeologist Reader, A250